LIVING IN FEAR IN CALIFORNIA

Living in Fear in California: How Well-Meaning Policy Mistakes Are Undermining Safe Communities and What Can Be Done to Restore Public Safety
By Kerry Jackson

May 2019

ISBN 978-1-934276-40-2

Pacific Research Institute
101 Montgomery Street, Suite 1300
San Francisco, CA 94104
Tel: 415-989-0833
Fax: 415-989-2411
www.pacificresearch.org

LIVING IN FEAR IN CALIFORNIA

How Well-Meaning Policy Mistakes Are Undermining Safe Communities and What Can Be Done to Restore Public Safety

By Kerry Jackson

PACIFIC RESEARCH INSTITUTE

Dedicated to the principle that protecting life, liberty, and property is one of government's few core duties, an enormous responsibility that can never be taken lightly.

Contents

Foreword
Sally C. Pipes
PRI President, CEO, and
Thomas W. Smith Fellow in Health Care Policy

From the 1980s through the 2000s, California was known as a state that had zero tolerance for serious and violent crime.

Legislative action and voter-approved initiatives enacted some of the nation's strongest public safety protections during this time frame. Crime rates fell across the state, and Californians felt safer in their homes, businesses, and communities. These policies proved successful in getting dangerous criminals off the streets and providing justice for crime victims and their families.

But these laws were almost too successful, and the state failed to increase prison capacity to correspond with the rising number of inmates. Since 1997, just 2 new state prison facilities have opened.

And then things changed – and dramatically – in the early 2010s. Faced with a court order to reduce prison overcrowding and a massive budget shortfall, the Legislature enacted former Governor Brown's public safety realignment plan in 2011. The plan shifted thousands of serious and repeat criminals from state prison to instead serve their time in local communities.

Along with three ballot measures enacted by voters – Propositions 36 (2012), 47 (2014), and 57 (2016) – these collective policy changes represented a radical departure from California's history of tough-on-crime policies.

Mr. Kerry Jackson, fellow with the Pacific Research Institute's Center for California Reform, explores each of these policy shifts in-depth and documents the impact each has had on California's communities.

He writes about car thefts and break-ins in San Francisco starting to accelerate from 2012 onward, violent crimes being underreported in Los Angeles, rising crime rates in San Jose (which was rated as one of the nation's safest big cities), rising incidents of metal theft in rural communities, and gang violence increasing across the state.

He also highlights local programs that are making a difference, such as a social media app in Sacramento that helps local police quickly address incidents of crime. Going beyond government, he also explores private sector anti-crime programs, including a private sector restorative justice program being targeted by San Francisco city officials that has been successful in reducing recidivism rates in shoplifters.

Jackson paints a portrait of well-meaning policy changes designed to reform our criminal justice system and reduce recidivism that have created big headaches for local law enforcement officials and put innocent people at risk of becoming a crime victim.

Most importantly, he outlines a series of reforms that lawmakers and policymakers should seriously consider as they address the unintended consequences of these laws and give law enforcement and prosecutors the tools they need to ensure justice is served.

Californians increasingly realize that something must be done to fix the problems triggered by these policy mistakes. Kerry Jackson's book is a welcome addition to the conversation that we hope will spur needed action to reform the law, so all Californians feel safe in their homes and communities again.

Chapter 1
California's Statewide Crime Problem Today

The façade of California's soft-on-crime approach leading to safer communities is starting to crack before our eyes. At its most fundamental level, government's role is to protect public safety but unfortunately, our state seems to be forgetting this core function.
– Andrea Seastrand
former member of Congress and current columnist
for the *San Luis Obispo Tribune*, March 3, 2018

At one time, California had a reputation for being hard on crime. It was not in another generation that Californians were said to support the harshest criminal sentencing system in the country, but in recent memory. The *Washington Post's* Max Ehrenfreund wrote in 2014 that "California's criminal justice system has long been among the most punitive."[1] Three years earlier, the *Huffington Post* remarked about "the state's 30-year legislative history of being tough on crime."[2] From the election of Ronald Reagan as governor in 1966 on a law-and-order platform, through the "three strikes" statute of 1994, named by *Newsweek* "the toughest law in the nation,"[3] to the administration of Democratic Governor Gray Davis, whom the *New York Times* declared in 2000 was "more of a conservative on criminal justice issues than his Republican predecessors,"[4] California was known as a state that had a low tolerance for criminal behavior.

When the late Governor George Deukmejian made his first inaugural address in 1983, he said that "All the prosperity in the world will not make our society better if our people are threatened by crime." At that time, violent crime in California was still on the rise while property crimes had peaked a few years earlier and were on their way down. By the early 1990s, the rates for both violent and property crimes were falling. Nationwide violent crime has fallen from 747.1 incidents per 100,000 residents in 1993[5] to 382.9 in 2017.[6] Property crime fell from 4,704 incidents per 100,000 residents in 1993[7] to 2,362.2 in 2017.[8]

But living in California today isn't quite as safe as we have come to expect it to be over the last two-and-a-half decades. After enjoying a decline in overall crime that began in 1993, California has grown more dangerous. By October 2014, the *Washington Post* was reporting that "California voters seem ready to end the state's 'tough on crime' era."[9] A month later, CBS News said California was going "from 'tough on crime' to 'let them go.'"[10]

At roughly the same time, violent crimes – measured by homicide, rape, robbery, aggravated assault – began to increase, while property crimes fell slightly in 2016 and 2017.[11]

For what it's worth, California was ranked as the 17th most dangerous state in the country based on the "number of violent and property crimes per capita."[12] Oakland was placed sixth in a 2019 list of the top 10 most dangerous cities in America.[13] A year earlier, California was ranked as the 13th most dangerous state.[14] In January 2018, three California cities were rated in the top 14 in a list of the 25 most dangerous cities in the country: Oakland (10th), Stockton (11th), and San Bernardino (14th).[15] All of these rankings are based on FBI data.

This book will look at the recent history of crime in California, review the trends, and provide snapshots through anecdotal material. It will examine the recent reforms that affect prison populations and sentencing, urban crime in the state's biggest cities, gang activity, rural crime, and violence in schools. Efforts to rehabilitate offenders, both by the government and private sector, as well as recidivism also will be analyzed. Finally, the book will offer reform recommendations to policymakers to address some of the state's most controversial and pressing crime issues.

Chapter 2
Urban Crime: Profiles of Crime in California's Major Cities

The key to safe neighborhoods is a partnership between police and community.
– Lt. Jason Clawson,
public information officer, Pasadena Police Department, December 5, 2017

LOS ANGELES

Violent crime in the city has followed the state trend, increasing in recent years after many years of decline. After falling to 16,524 incidents in 2013, from 52,243 in 2000, incidents of violent crime have risen in recent years to 30,507 in 2017.[16]

Meanwhile, property crimes increased for the fourth straight year in 2017.[17] In 2018, vehicle break-ins spiked in the first half of the year. There were 893 through July 14, nearly 30 percent more than the 690 break-ins over the same period in 2017.[18]

AFTER YEARS OF DECLINE, VIOLENT CRIME IN LA SURGING

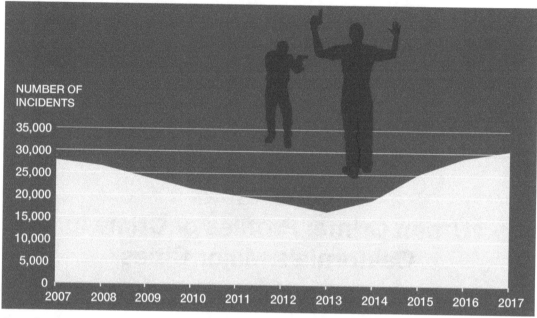

Source: Open Justice, California Department of Justice, Data Exploration, Crime Statistics, Crimes and Clearances

PROPERTY CRIME IN LA ALSO ON RISE AFTER YEARS OF DECLINE

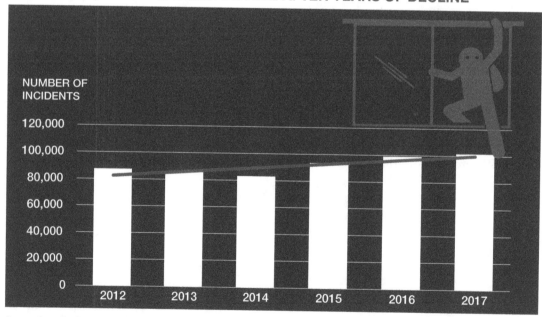

Source: Open Justice, California Department of Justice, Data Exploration, Crime Statistics, Crimes and Clearances

The true number of criminal incidents, however, especially those of an aggravated nature, might have been considerably higher during a period beginning in the late-mid-2000s through the middle of the 2010s. The *Los Angeles Times* reported in October 2015 that the Los Angeles Police Department had been underreporting serious assaults, which distorted crime statistics for nearly a decade. According to the newspaper's analysis, police "misclassified an estimated 14,000 serious assaults as minor offenses in a recent eight-year period, artificially lowering the city's crime levels."

"With the incidents counted correctly, violent crime in the city was 7 percent higher than the LAPD reported in the period from 2005 to fall 2012, and the number of serious assaults was 16 percent higher, the analysis found."[19]

The *Times* provided an example of the underreporting. Police said that in 2009, April L. Taylor stabbed her boyfriend in the stomach with a kitchen knife during a domestic dispute, but the incident was not logged in as it should have been.

"Police arrested Taylor, who later was found guilty of assault with a deadly weapon. In the LAPD's crime database, however, the attack was recorded as a 'simple assault.' Because of this, the case—like other misclassified incidents—was left out of the department's tally of violence in the city."[20]

> **The *Los Angeles Times* reported in October 2015 that the Los Angeles Police Department had been underreporting serious assaults, which distorted crime statistics for nearly a decade.**

The *Times*' 2014 investigation "found that the LAPD misclassified nearly 1,200 violent crimes during a one-year span ending in September 2013." Beatings, stabbings and robberies that should have been documented as aggravated assaults "instead were recorded as minor offenses." Had they been appropriately logged in, "the figures for aggravated assaults in the year-long period would have been nearly 14 percent higher, the *Times* found."[21]

The newspaper also found that from 2005 to fall 2012, the LAPD misclassified an estimated 14,000 aggravated assaults as minor offenses, artificially lowering the city's violent crime rate. After the *Times*' reports, a 2015 audit by the LAPD's inspector general estimated the department misclassified more than 25,000 aggravated assaults as minor incidents from 2008 to 2014.[22]

In the fall of 2017, a captain from the Los Angeles Police Department's Van Nuys station filed a lawsuit against the city, alleging that crimes in the Foothill area had been underreported, and that she had been conveying her concerns to supervisors about the issue since 2014. "After assuming command of the Van Nuys station in 2015," the *Los Angeles Times* reported, Captain Lillian Carranza "conducted her own analysis of violent crime reports stored in an LAPD database, according to the claim."[23]

Aggravated assaults in 2016 were underreported by about 10 percent in the Pacific and Central divisions, according to the claim, which alleges that those cases were misclassified as less serious offenses.

The LAPD, according to Carranza's complaint, "engaged in a highly complex and elaborate coverup in an attempt to hide the fact that command officers had been providing false crime figures to the public attempting to convince the public that crime was not significantly increasing."[24]

Carranza has also said the aggravated assaults in the Hollenbeck and Mission divisions were underreported by 10 percent.

Aggravated assaults in the Pacific and Central divisions were underreported by 10 percent in 2016, according to Carranza's suit.

Police officials explained that "classification errors are inevitable in a department that records more than 100,000 serious offenses each year." Police Chief Charlie Beck said properly classifying crimes is "a complex process that is subject to human error."[25] But there are suspicions that crimes were intentionally mislabeled to make the department look like it was doing more to reduce serious crime than it was.

"If the misclassifications were mainly inadvertent, police would be expected to make a similar number of mistakes in each direction — reporting serious crimes as minor ones and vice versa, Eli Silverman, professor emeritus at John Jay College of Criminal Justice in New York," told the *Times*.[26]

"But the *Times'* review found that when police miscoded crimes, the result nearly always was to turn a serious crime into a minor one."[27]

The *Los Angeles Daily News* reported in November 2017 that an audit conducted in 2015 "by an independent watchdog of the department" found that a "significant number" of crimes that had been categorized as simple assaults from 2008-2014 "were actually aggravated assaults and should have been included as part of the violent crime statistics that are submitted to the FBI and disclosed to the public."[28]

"The Office of the Inspector General," said the *Los Angeles Daily News*, "found that if the crimes had been classified correctly during those seven years, the rate of aggravated assaults reported to the FBI and the public would have been an average of 36 percent higher."[29]

SAN FRANCISCO

Violent crime peaked in 2013, with 7,064 incidents, then fell for three years before rising in 2017. Homicides increased in recent years to 57 in 2016, then falling by one in 2017. Rapes exploded in 2014 with 355, more than double the year before, then decreased slightly in 2015 and 2016 before rising to 367 in 2017. Robberies and aggravated assault both trended downward in recent years after growing earlier in the decade.[30]

INCIDENTS OF RAPE HAVE TRIPLED IN SAN FRANCISCO, DESPITE HOMICIDE RATES FALLING BY HALF

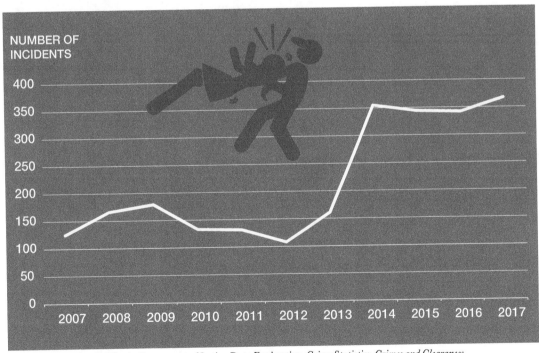

Source: Open Justice, California Department of Justice, Data Exploration, Crime Statistics, Crimes and Clearances

Meanwhile, car break-ins in San Francisco have become a major nuisance. They were up by about one-fourth in 2017 over 2016. More than 30,000 were reported in 2017, almost three times the number reported in 2010.[31] The incidents have risen so sharply that in 2015, San Francisco had the highest increase in property crimes of any city in the U.S., according to FBI statistics.[32]

Max Szabo, spokesman for the San Francisco District Attorney said in February 2018 that the wave of automobile break-ins had reached the level of an "epidemic."[33] Victims have felt "violated," "helpless," and "aggravated."[34] One resignedly said that being a victim is "part of city living."[35]

SAN FRANCISCO HAS FACED WAVE OF AUTOMOBILE BREAK-INS

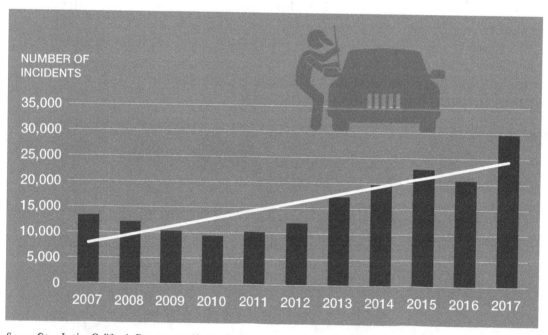

Source: Open Justice, California Department of Justice, Data Exploration, Crime Statistics, Crimes and Clearances

Several theories have been floated to explain the rise, according to KQED News:

> Cars are packed close together, and it's easy to break into one car after another.

> We have a lot of tourists who leave stuff in their cars out of necessity, or because they aren't aware of the break-in threat.

> The things we leave in our cars have gotten more expensive over the years. Burglars once stole CD players—now they steal laptops.[36]

Arrests for breaking into cars are rare. Arrests are made in only 2 percent of reported incidents.[37] To step up enforcement, San Francisco District Attorney George Gascón proposed in February 2018 a $1 million task force as "a way for all of us to come together and to make sure that we end this problem this year."[38]

SAN DIEGO

Violent crime in one of only two big cities in the state with a Republican mayor has been falling generally, with upticks in 2012 and 2015, then decreasing in 2016 and 2017. Homicides, which increased in 2015 and 2016, fell by 30 percent in 2017. Rape grew for five straight years, then declined in 2017, while robbery has risen for four consecutive years. Aggravated assault increased from 2013 to 2015, then fell in 2016 and 2017.[39]

On a Saturday night in early February 2018, three people were shot in two separate incidents in south San Diego communities just two miles apart. All were hospitalized for non-life-threatening injuries.[40] Later in the month, 27-year-old Alexander Mazin was shot to death in a 24-Hour Fitness parking lot off Midway Drive on a Sunday morning.[41]

Not quite a year earlier, a gunman killed one and injured seven others at a pool party in an apartment complex near La Jolla in what then-San Diego Police Chief Shelley Zimmerman called a "rampage." The suspect, 49-year-old Peter Selis, was later shot and killed by police.[42]

SAN DIEGO HOMICIDE NUMBERS FELL IN 2017 AFTER CLIMBING FOR THREE YEARS

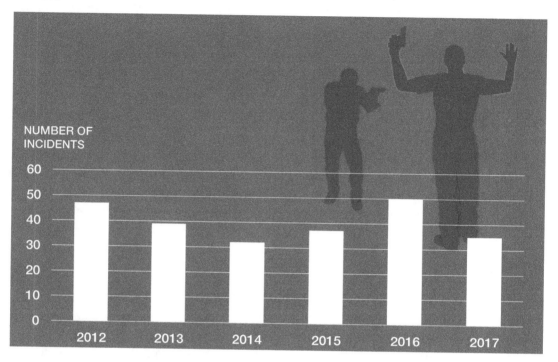

Source: *Open Justice, California Department of Justice, Data Exploration, Crime Statistics, Crimes and Clearances*

Despite events such as these, crime is becoming less common in San Diego. City officials announced in early 2018 that crime had hit a 49-year low the year before, down 7 percent. Murders in 2017 had fallen to 34 from 50 in 2016, a 32 percent drop, rape from 572 incidents to 559, and assault from 5,332 to 5,221. Robbery increased slightly, up to 1,410 incidents from 1,387. Total violent crimes declined from 5,332 to 5,221, a 2 percent decrease.[43]

Burglaries dropped 20 percent in 2017, to 3,817 from 4,743, while thefts decreased to 17,294 from 18,042, and motor vehicle thefts from 5,839 to 5,135. Overall property crimes fell 8 percent, from 28,624 to 26,246.[44]

PROPERTY CRIMES IN SAN DIEGO HAVE FALLEN SHARPLY SINCE 2007

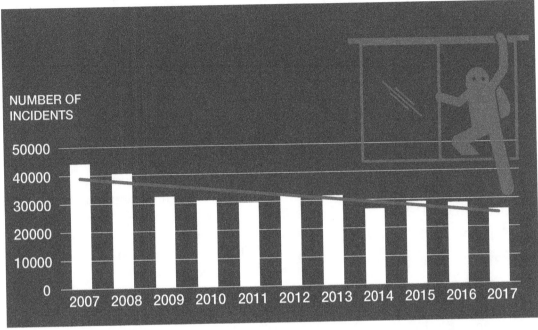

Source: Open Justice, California Department of Justice, Data Exploration, Crime Statistics, Crimes and Clearances

Before these data were compiled, San Diego was named the safest big city in the country for murders. There were 3.5 murders per 100,000 residents in the city of San Diego and just three murders per 100,000 in San Diego County. The next safest big cities were New York, with 3.9 murders per 100,000, and San Jose, with 4.5. The national rate is 5.3 murders per 100,000 residents.[45]

Law enforcement officials haven't pointed to any single reason crime has fallen in San Diego, in part because it's simply too early to know. One possibility, though, is that the police department has at the same time become more aggressive and more diplomatic within the community.

"If there's a violent crime in the area, we are flooding that area," said San Diego Police Lt. Manny Del Toro. "I mean, we are literally turning over stones. We're stopping a lot of people. The heat is on."[46]

Meanwhile, the department is also ensuring that "people have a better understanding of why we do what we do" so that there "will be less friction between officers on the job and community members," said Del Toro.[47] "It has slowly become more accepted that when crimes are committed, yeah, we are going to be out in force."[48]

The San Diego Police Department has partnered with the private sector through the Community Assistance Support Team, which acts as a channel between law enforcement and communities, particularly those where a distrust of authorities exists. Bishop Cornelius Bowser, a Community Assistance Support Team leader and pastor at Charity Apostolic Church, has said that it is important for law enforcement "to put more time, effort and resources into building public trust and legitimacy in the community."

San Diego police have also employed technology to help fight crime. ShotSpotter, a gunshot detection technology that uses sophisticated acoustic sensors to detect, locate and alert law enforcement agencies and security personnel about illegal gunfire incidents in real-time,[49] according to the company's description, has been employed in San Diego since late 2016. Police officials said a little more than a year later, the system was especially helpful in allowing law enforcement to respond to shots that would otherwise go unreported.

> **The San Diego Police Department has partnered with the private sector through the Community Assistance Support Team, which acts as a channel between law enforcement and communities, particularly those where a distrust of authorities exists.**

"The great thing about this technology is that 100 percent of the time, not only did we get notified" that there had been gunfire, "but we responded — and to a more precise location," Zimmerman said. Del Toro said that without ShotSpotter "officers can sometimes spend a lot of time going door-to-door trying to figure out where a shooting might have happened." The technology, he said, "can definitely save some time."[50]

In the case of a shooting in the Encanto neighborhood in November 2017, police were already on their way by the time nearby residents had gotten through to 911 operators.[51]

While crime is down, there remains a pocket of trouble in the Pacific Beach neighborhood, a "beachside entertainment hotspot" just south of La Jolla and north of Mission Bay. "Public records indicate the beachside entertainment hotspot ranked in the top five in rapes, assaults, and home and auto thefts last year," the *San Diego Reader* reported in February 2018. "During 2017, the police department logged 26 rape cases in Pacific Beach, only one behind East Village during the same time. . . . In regard to aggravated assaults, Pacific Beach again finished second to East Village with 113 reported cases."[52]

Pacific Beach had the highest incidence of residential and non-residential burglaries for any San Diego neighborhood, and the second-highest number of car thefts.[53]

"A lot of the residents in Pacific Beach are just fed up and we want some law changes and that's the only way some of these criminals are going to be dealt with properly," Racheal Allen said in April 2018.

Allen is one of many neighbors looking for a solution to the increasing crime who are "banding together by introducing a measure called Keep Cal Safe that would enact tougher laws to keep repeat offenders off the streets." The measure will appear on the November 2020 ballot.[54]

"There is a lot of crime that is considered non-violent which should be re-classified as violent," said Allen.

OAKLAND

Paul Vasconcelos, manager of Crown Liquors in the upscale neighborhood of Montclair, recalls "a guy I saw going by across the street, pulling door handles. He couldn't get into the cars. He left."[55] What Vasconcelos likely witnessed was a part of the wave of automobile break-ins that have also been afflicting San Francisco.

Violent crime in Oakland, however, has been trending downward for five years. It's as low as it has been in more than 10 years. The city issued a statement in January 2018 that read:

> The FBI's violent crime index – which tracks murders, rape, robbery, and assault – has dropped 23 percent in Oakland from 2012 to 2017, with the steepest declines in shootings (down 50 percent) homicides (down 42 percent) and robbery (down 38 percent) during that time frame.
>
> In 2012, the city saw 553 shootings and 125 homicides. By comparison, in 2017 the city witnessed 277 shootings and 72 homicides – Oakland's second lowest homicide total since records were kept in 1985."[56]

Homicides declined in 2017 to 72 from 85 in 2016 (which doesn't include the 36 deaths from the December 2016 Ghost Ship warehouse fire), while injuries from shootings declined from 331 in 2016 to 277 in 2017.[57] Overall violent crime decreased 5 percent in 2017 over 2016.[58]

DECLINE IN VIOLENT CRIME HAS MADE OAKLAND A SAFER CITY

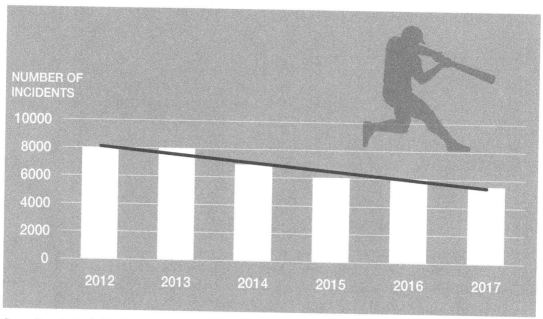

Source: *Open Justice, California Department of Justice, Data Exploration, Crime Statistics, Crimes and Clearances*

    The *San Francisco Chronicle* reported that "city police leaders attributed the drop in 2017 to a community program that, among other goals, seeks to intervene in gang disputes and help troubled youths before they commit shootings."[59]

    "I can tell you, the last five years, we've seen an enormous paradigm shift in regard to how we police and are part of this community," said Oakland Police Capt. Ersie Joyner III, who commands Ceasefire, "a data-driven violence-reduction strategy coordinating law enforcement, social services, and the community" designed to "reduce gang/group-related homicides and shootings"[60] that was introduced in 2012. "No longer are the days of doing random police work. We have a laser focus on trying to identify, using data, the individuals who are most at risk for being involved in gun violence or being engaged in gun violence."[61]

    Yet the quality of life is still strained in some neighborhoods due to property crimes.

AUTOMOBILE BREAK-INS RAPIDLY ON RISE IN OAKLAND

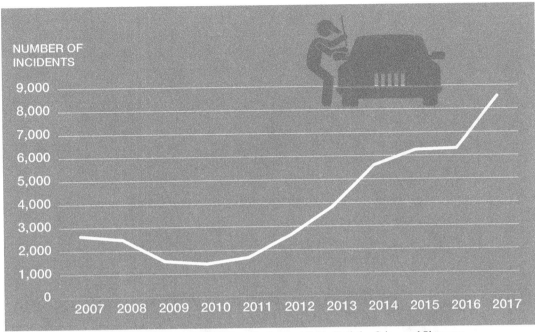

NUMBER OF
INCIDENTS

| | 2007 | 2008 | 2009 | 2010 | 2011 | 2012 | 2013 | 2014 | 2015 | 2016 | 2017 |

Source: *Open Justice, California Department of Justice, Data Exploration, Crime Statistics, Crimes and Clearances*

"It's really an alarming increase and I have a feeling it's only going to get worse," Bradley White, a Montclair homeowner says. "When I leave my car, will my window be broken, is my car even going to be there?"[62]

Another Montclair resident, Dianne Noroian, has told the story of her family being victimized four times – two car break-ins and two cars stolen. The experience has forced her and her husband to change the way they live. "My husband gets up every morning to see if any of our cars have windows that have been smashed," Noroian said. "Before we leave the house, I take all of my computers and lock them away."[63]

In January 2018, an employee of a neighborhood grocery store confronted a shop-lifting suspect. He was fired for his trouble, leaving residents feeling even more vulnerable. One neighbor said "people are outraged" by the firing. Reporter Juliette Goodrich of KPIX-TV said she had been told that employees "had seen this kind of rise in shoplifting ever since customers are asked to bring in their own bags . . . they fill up the bags and leave without going through the check register."[64]

KTVU-TV news reported that "residents says they want the employee reinstated and they'd like to see more police presence in the area."[65]

SACRAMENTO

In the Pocket-Greenhaven neighborhood, which experienced the largest decrease in violent crime in 2017 over 2016, residents have taken it upon themselves to keep the peace.

"Will Cannady, the president of the Pocket Greenhaven Community Association, credits the active engagement among residents and frequent reporting to the neighborhood's NextDoor social media page for the low violent crime rates," the *Sacramento Bee* reported in February 2018. Sacramento Police spokesman Eddie Macaulay attributed the decrease to "the relationships that we have with the community groups, the citizens," which "go a long way to reduce crime in the city."[66] Sacramento City Councilman Jay Schenirer said that he believes "the safety of a community is in the hands of the community."[67]

Property crime in the neighborhood, however, rose 4.1 percent in 2017.[68] Across the city, though, violent crime fell 5.4 percent while property crime dropped 5.3 percent. Crime overall decreased by 5.3 percent.

SACRAMENTO HOMICIDE NUMBERS HAVE FALLEN AFTER A 2015 SURGE

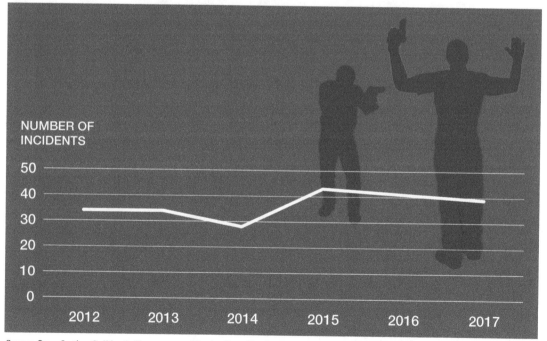

NUMBER OF INCIDENTS

Source: *Open Justice, California Department of Justice, Data Exploration, Crime Statistics, Crimes and Clearances*

As of November 2017, 160 neighborhoods and 80,000 members were using Next-Door in Sacramento.[69] The Sacramento Police Department's use of social media goes back to 2009, when it began to use Facebook and Twitter. Officer.com explains the department's two-fold approach through social media begins with building a relationship with the community, then using that connection to share information that goes in both directions.[70]

NextDoor, which describes itself as "a private social network for your neighborhood," provides law enforcement with a platform in which it can post crime and security notices that can be read by residents, who can then respond to them. Residents can also post information, complaints and photographs on the site, giving officers an advantage they hadn't had previously. Communication is instant, which allows officers to act quicker than they had been able to in the past.

"Years ago, we maybe needed a tip to come in and it could be weeks before it got to us," Sacramento Police Capt. Bill Champion Jr. has said. "The fact that citizens are more involved gets us more information."[71]

SAN JOSE

The heart of Silicon Valley, which has promoted itself as one of the safest big cities in the country, has been experiencing an upsurge in violent crime. Homicides, aggravated assaults, rapes and robberies rose 7 percent in 2017, following a 14 percent increase in 2016, according to San Jose Police Department data.

Mayor Sam Liccardo said that, "It doesn't matter that we're still among the safest large cities in the nation. We see a rising trend of violent crime, and we have ample reason to be concerned and respond immediately."[72]

Liccardo cited increases in youth and gang-related crimes as reasons for the rise in violent crime. Mario Maciel, superintendent of the Mayor's Gang Prevention Task Force, said many of the young offenders are not affiliated with gangs. "I'm seeing some nontraditional groupings. These kids are organizing on the internet to commit a rash of robberies."[73]

> The heart of Silicon Valley, which has promoted itself as one of the safest big cities in the country, has been experiencing an upsurge in violent crime.

In some instances, young adults, not much beyond their 18th birthdays, are working with juveniles to commit crimes. A robbery crew arrested in January 2018, made up of seven adults and five juveniles, was suspected in 30 San Jose robberies and carjackings.[74]

Three high-speed chases in November 2017 resulted in the arrests of 11 juveniles, one as young as 11, for a series of armed carjackings, burglaries and robberies, adult crimes allegedly committed by minors over a six-hour period. The *Sacramento Bee* reported that "Victims have said in the past the lenient juvenile justice laws may be part of the problem." Victim Robert Moore told a local television station "that his house was ransacked by a juvenile suspect — but when the suspect was apprehended, the suspect was only behind bars a few days."[75]

"There's some serious holes in the system that these young offenders are exploiting, knowing they're going to be able to get away with what they are doing," San Jose police Sgt. Sean Pritchard told a local station.[76]

> The capital of Silicon Valley still is not the South Side of Chicago. The numbers of crimes remain low for a city of a million people.

A *San Jose Mercury News* editorial characterized the "wild percentage increases" in crimes "might imply the city is overrun by rampaging teen-age Huns." But it also noted that "The capital of Silicon Valley still is not the South Side of Chicago. The numbers of crimes remain low for a city of a million people. Oakland, with an estimated 426,000 residents, still averages 1 1/2 times the amount of violent crime as San Jose," (a data point attributed to the community-policing strategies used by San Jose.) Yet there still exist some "unnerving trends," which the editorial board believes can be reversed by the "community-policing strategies that have helped Oakland and East Palo Alto get crime under control in recent years (and) are the ones that help keep San Jose a pretty safe city."[77]

SMALLER CITIES

The largest increases in violent crime over the first six months of 2017 were not in the state's biggest cities but in Glendale (35 percent), Victorville (30 percent), Pomona (26 percent), Berkeley (22 percent), Garden Grove (22 percent), and Huntington Beach (20 percent).[78] Of these cities, only Victorville is located outside of a major metropolitan region.

"Data analysis by the Criminal Justice Legal Foundation found that, of the 73 California cities listed in the" 2017 FBI Preliminary Semiannual Crime Report, "56 percent had an increase in violent crime."[79]

There were 274 violent crimes – homicides, robberies, rapes, and aggravated assaults – in Glendale in all of 2017, police say, compared to 229 in 2016,[80] which was 17 percent higher than 2015.[81]

In the entirety of 2017, violent crime in Victorville was up 9 percent compared to 2016, which had an increase of 8 percent over 2015. "Over the past few years, several new laws have been implemented that continue to present many challenges to law enforcement and have made it increasingly difficult for us to do our job," Victorville Police Chief John McMahon said in early 2018.[82]

In Pomona, "the Mexican Mafia had 'total control' of street gangs" in the city until "an expansive sweep" there and in other Los Angeles County municipalities took dozens of gang suspects off the streets in May 2018.[83]

Berkeley finished 2017 with a 12 percent increase in violent crime, on top of an 18 percent increase in 2016, and a 20 percent rise in 2015.[84] In Huntington Beach, incidents of violent crime rose from 360 in 2016 to 461 in 2017, an increase of 28 percent.[85]

The most hazardous mid-size city in California might be Stockton. The National Council for Home Safety and Security ranks the city ninth in its top 10 most dangerous cities in the country with more than 100,000 residents.[86] After falling sharply in 2013, violent crime rates have increased every year since to 4,381 in 2016, then decreasing by two to 4,379 in 2017. Homicides and robberies have also increased every year after dropping through 2013.[87]

The most hazardous mid-size city in California might be Stockton.

Stockton has decided that the best way to reduce the violence is to hand out "stipends of up to $1,000 a month to residents deemed most likely to shoot somebody."[88]

"This program is called Advance Peace, and it's modeled after a crime reduction program in the Bay Area city of Richmond," the *Los Angeles Times* reported in May 2018. "The idea is that a small number of people are responsible for a large percentage of violence, and offering them an alternative path – with counseling and case management over an 18-month period, along with a stipend if they stay the course – can be a good investment all around."[89]

The pilot program, financed by a nonprofit partnership, is not a new idea – even Richard Nixon gave some consideration to a universal basic income – nor is the idea solely associated with only one side of the political aisle. But the hope of paying violent people to be peaceful seems more aspirational than rational. And even should it succeed, it will still be a failure because it would create a moral hazard. Policymakers would be unrelenting in their efforts to find other bad behaviors for which they could pay potential offenders to refrain from committing.

Chapter 3
Rural Crime in California

As a cattleman and a peace officer, I see firsthand the impact that rural crime has on California farmers and ranchers as their equipment, livestock and crops are either stolen or damaged each year, resulting in untold losses to rural communities.
– Yuba Community College District Police Chief John Osbourn,
AgAlert, June 10, 2015

Santa Barbara County Sheriff's Deputy John McCarthy has an unusual job. As a member of the county's Rural Crime Unit, he has driven the lonely back roads of the county to uphold the law. On some days he'd drive as many as 200 miles.[90]

"Farmers and ranchers are hard-working, honest people," he told the *Santa Maria Sun*. "When somebody targets them, and they become a victim of a crime, I take it personally. I'll bend over backwards to make sure I do an investigation as thorough as I can."[91] The Rural Crime Unit chases mushroom poachers, fuel-theft rings, tractor thieves, fertilizer filchers, avocado pirates, and generator bandits.

"You name it on a farm, it gets stolen," McCarthy said. Of particular interest to rural raiders is wire and other metals. Copper cable is especially valuable and is often yanked out of irrigation pumps, rendering them useless. Without working pumps, fields can flood, and crops can become parched.

If you're farming or ranching in California, there's a good chance you've been the victim of metal theft or know someone who has, says the California Farm Bureau. From copper wire to brass valves to aluminum irrigation pipe, crooks are attacking at an alarming rate and doing a considerable amount of damage along the way.

The story is a familiar one: A farmer checks his pump in preparation for irrigating and finds that the copper wire has been stripped and there is no way to provide water to the fields. He makes the loop, checking all of the pumps on the property and learns he has been the victim of copper theft at multiple locations. Thieves have stripped the pumps in order to recycle the wire at the local scrap yard. Thieves might get only a few hundred dollars for stolen metal while leaving their victim facing a repair bill of $1,500 to $4,000 or more for each pump.[92]

The Legislature enacted several bills aimed at curbing metal theft, notably Assembly Bill 844 and Senate Bill 447, both in 2008. AB 844 requires recyclers to keep detailed records of purchases and payments while SB 447 requires that the records be regularly reported to local law enforcement agencies.

"Both of these laws have helped play a role in reducing metal theft rates that have had negative impacts on farmers and ranchers throughout the state," says Noelle Cremers of the California Farm Bureau Federation. "During the height of the metal theft epidemic, our members regularly saw copper wire ripped out of pumps, which provided the thieves with $20 worth of metal while causing thousands of dollars in damages to the pump." [93]

Some rural residents believe that many crimes are simply going unreported.

But the value of these laws, she added, "is only as strong as their enforcement, and with shifts in law enforcement priorities, metal theft is not always the top priority. When they are enforced, they can make a real difference. For example, one recycler agreed to a $4.1 million fine in 2013 after it was found the business was buying stolen metal and not following the law regarding record keeping and payment requirements." [94]

While crime rates were still falling in late 2011, Victor Davis Hanson wrote that "I am starting to feel as if I am living in a Vandal state, perhaps on the frontier near Carthage around A.D. 530, or in a beleaguered Rome in 455." The stories he told *National Review* are discouraging.

Last week an ancestral rural school near the Kings River had its large bronze bell stolen. I think it dated from 1911. I have driven by it about 100 times in the 42 years since I got my first license. The bell had endured all those years. Where it is now I don't know. Does someone just cut up a beautifully crafted bell in some chop yard in rural Fresno County, without a worry about who forged it or why — or why others for a century until now enjoyed its presence?

The (nearby) city of Fresno is now under siege. Hundreds of street lights are out, their copper wire stripped away. In desperation, workers are now cementing the bases of all the poles — as if the original steel access doors were not necessary to service the wiring. How sad the synergy! Since darkness begets crime, the thieves achieve a twofer: The more copper they steal, the easier under cover of spreading night it is to steal more.

In a small town two miles away, the thefts now sound like something out of Edward Gibbon's bleaker chapters — or maybe George Miller's "Road Warrior," or the Hughes brothers' more recent "The Book of Eli." Hundreds of bronze commemorative plaques were ripped off my town's public buildings (and with them all record of our ancestors' public-spiritedness). I guess that is our version of Trotskyization.

The Catholic church was just looted (again) of its bronze and silver icons. Manhole covers are missing (some of the town's own maintenance staff were arrested for this theft, no less!). The Little League clubhouse was ransacked of its equipment.[95]

Hanson said, "there is indeed something of the Dark Ages about all this" and lamented that "when we leave for a trip or just go into town, the predators swarm."[96]

Some rural residents believe that many crimes are simply going unreported. Hanson said in his experience rural Californians believe 75 percent of crime in their areas goes unreported either because the residents "know the authorities are short-handed or that little will be done to those if caught."[97]

While the public often associates crime and victimization with urban cores, "large, sparsely populated areas in rural California are also considered attractive venues for criminals," says Taylor Roschen of the California Farm Bureau Federation, and "underreporting will continue to exacerbate the issue."

"Farmers, ranchers and agricultural businesses often become victimized by vandalism, theft, and drug-related crimes, which may not be abated through the conventional methods used by law enforcement in urban areas," Roschen says. "It's also worth noting that 'underreporting' includes not reporting the true dollar value of the stolen or damaged property, which is often difficult for agriculturalists to quantify."[98]

There are many reasons for the underreporting, according to Roschen. Among them are a lack of confidence in restitution, a burden to report that is greater than the valuation of the loss, slow response rates, and "even a lack of knowledge by a property owner that a crime has occurred."

Rural crime has become an increasing problem in the state and poor reporting, whether it is of the actual crimes or the true value of the property losses, has only masked its severity.

"Another factor that plays a role: As California addresses criminal-justice reform, legislative remedies and voter-led initiatives have often positioned rural crimes as 'wobblers,' where they can be pled down to or charged as misdemeanors or a citation rather than felonies – or as the criminal justice system becomes overloaded and district attorneys' caseloads expand, there is simply a lack of appetite to prosecute."[99]

Rural crime has become an increasing problem in the state and poor reporting, whether it is of the actual crimes or the true value of the property losses, has only masked its severity.

Chapter 4
Beyond the Crips and Bloods:
California's Gang Crime Problem

Los Angeles has long been recognized as the epicenter of gang activity nationwide. . . .
Many gangs which today have a nationwide presence, such as the Bloods, the Crips,
Mara Salvatrucha (MS-13), and 18th Street, can trace their roots to Los Angeles.
– FBI Special Agent Robert B. Loosle, 2006 Congressional testimony.

Early in the morning of Jan. 5, 2018, a couple of hours after midnight, 21-year-old Anthony Escobedo was shot to death in Bell Gardens, a city of 42,000 just southeast of Los Angeles. Officials identified Escobedo as a gang member.[100]

Six months earlier, in July 2017, a male, "estimated to be in his late teens or early 20s," was found dead on the street in South Los Angeles around 11:30 p.m. on a weekday. The "known gang-member" "died from a gunshot wound to the head."[101] In the fall of the year, a senior from Palos Verdes High School, who comes from an affluent family and lived in a suburban neighborhood not known for criminal or gang activity, was charged with murder for being the alleged getaway driver in a fatal gang shooting. Officials said Cameron Terrell, then 18, was part of a group that killed 21-year-old Justin Alongino Holmes in South Los Angeles.[102]

These are common events in the metropolitan Los Angeles area. But they are less common than they once were.

First, some background. The Los Angeles Police Department says that the city and county of Los Angeles is the "gang capital" of the country. There are more than 450 active gangs, with a combined membership of roughly 45,000. Many of the gangs have existed for more than 50 years.[103]

The LAPD has not released complete data on gang-related crime since 2009, and the county hasn't since 2012.[104] A note on the Los Angeles Police Department website in May 2018 said "Gang stats for 2010-2015 are unavailable at this time. When they become available, they will be posted here."[105]

In January 2018, Los Angeles police officials reported that gang-related homicides increased 13 percent in 2017 over 2016.[106] Overall gang crime jumped 14.6 percent in 2015, the first increase in eight years, Los Angeles Police Chief Charlie Beck said in January 2016.[107] In 2015, almost 60 percent of the 283 homicides in the city were associated with gang violence.[108]

TABLE 1: GANG-RELATED VS. NON-GANG-RELATED HOMICIDES IN LOS ANGELES

	GANG-RELATED	NON-GANG-RELATED
2017	177	105
2016	157	137
2015	165	118

Source: Los Angeles Police Department, Homicide Report 2017

Before those documented increases, it was thought that gang crime was falling in Los Angeles. But Sam Quinones, author, former *Los Angeles Times* reporter and a national authority on gangs, says that was more of a case of lowered visibility.

"Gangs have moved off the streets, moved indoors, are far more discreet and low profile than they were during their many years of infamy," from the 1960s through the early 2000s, he said in February 2015.[109]

"They're still involved in crime – burglary, jewelry heists, identity theft and, of course, various forms of drug trafficking. But they're not the classic 'street' gangs of yesteryear that created so much havoc and destruction in their working-class and poor neighborhoods."[110]

Quinones later wrote about, "the daily degradation and intimidation of whole neighborhoods — the carjackings, graffiti, shootings and, of course, the constant hanging out — is no longer central to how they operate." He noted that parks which had once been notorious gang hangouts "have been returned to their rightful owners: neighborhood residents."[111] Three years later, in January 2018, Quinones wrote:

Gangs have largely stopped the public behavior that did so much to crush working-class neighborhoods. Families in those neighborhoods don't face the risk to their children they once did. Business owners no longer have massive graffiti to paint over every month.

Homeowners in black and Latino neighborhoods are now able to unlock the value of their homes – in both sales and home-equity loans – in a way that was impossible a decade ago. Gangs, after all, were always the best rent control.[112]

Quinones credited a "new" Los Angeles Police Department that "is one of the most transformed institutions in California civic life in the last 25 years."[113] Others believe that "gang injunctions" have helped. According to the Los Angeles Police Department:

A gang injunction is a restraining order against a group. It is a civil suit that seeks a court order declaring the gang's public behavior a nuisance and asking for special rules directed toward its activity. Injunctions can address the neighborhood's gang problem before it reaches the level of felony crime activity.[114]

The *Los Angeles Times* calls them "court orders that restrict the activity of particular people in designated neighborhoods in the name of curbing gang violence."[115]

Los Angeles Police Department use of gang injunctions sharply increased in the 1980s and 1990s, which were marked by historically high gang violence. Multiple studies determined that gang injunctions reduced gang crime, including one entitled "Evaluation of the Effectiveness of Gang Injunctions in California." It found that:

Part 1 (violent crime) calls decreased 11.6 percent compared to base-line, while controls averaged an increase of 0.8 percent, a net benefit of 12.4 percent. Part 2 (less serious) calls decreased 15.9 percent compared to base-line, while controls averaged a mild increase of 1.6 percent, a net benefit of 17.5 percent.[116]

Critics complained that law enforcement eventually went too far, using gang injunctions as a shortcut and violating the rights of those named in the injunctions to freely move about. The practice came under increasing criticism by 2016, which roughly coincides with the rise in gang crime. The American Civil Liberties Union sued the city over gang injunctions that same year. In March 2018 Chief U.S. District Judge Virginia A. Phillips barred the city from enforcing gang injunctions.[117]

Though the *Los Angeles Times* cited in a March 2018 editorial the "blunt misuse of gang injunctions" and the overstepping of "constitutional bounds," it also urged the city to "keep gang injunctions in L.A.'s crime-fighting toolbox."[118] Said the *Times* editorial board:

> A constitutional gang injunction would provide adequate prior notice to its target and would establish in court, beyond a reasonable doubt, that the person is involved in gang activity. It would be time-limited and would provide adequate opportunity for the subject to seek removal, by following criteria approved in court.
>
> Ending injunctions would send the pendulum swinging too far in the other direction. There is no reason for the city not to keep its crime-fighting tools well-honed and up to date. Nor is there any reason to believe that they cannot craft those tools carefully, so that they comply with the Constitution and respect the dignity and the civil rights of the people to be covered.[119]

South of Los Angeles in Orange County, parents say "they don't let their children play outside because they live in neighborhoods dominated by gangs and drugs," according to the *Orange County Register.* "One mother said she doesn't go out at night, even if she needs milk or bread. Another said her children worry when she takes a walk, fearing she might get shot."[120]

There are an estimated 13,000 gang members in Orange County, with some of the highest concentrations in Santa Ana and Anaheim. That's down significantly, though, from the mid-1990s when the estimate was 19,000.[121] The decline coincides with the development of the Orange County Gang Reduction Intervention Partnership (OCGRIP). The organization, begun in 2008 by the Orange County District Attorney's office with the cooperation of the Orange County Sheriff's Department, and funded by donations from the private sector and litigation settlements, has been called a "national model for preventing gang membership" by Jim Bueermann, president of the Police Foundation and a former Redlands police chief.[122] Bueermann wrote about the Police Foundation's assessment of the program:

> Our research evaluated OCGRIP's premise targeting fourth- through eighth-grade students in targeted schools who have displayed behavior indicating risk for later gang involvement.

Our Phase I findings validate OCGRIP's premise that truancy is an early indicator of future gang membership. In one school we documented a 100% reduction in truancy — a key marker in the program's success.

In addition, our analysis emphasized the significant impact that incentives (provided by the business community and others) have on youth motivation and hope. They specifically credited the creative inputs of mentors, volunteers, police, and the business community as key program supporters and contributors to the program's success. In sum, we found that the program effectively balances enforcement with compassion in preventing gang membership and promoting youth success.[123]

At the beginning of the 2017-18 school year, more than 900 fourth- through eighth-grade Orange County students were identified as being at the greatest risk of joining a gang. They were challenged by OCGRIP to improve their school attendance, to avoid behavior that would result in disciplinary action, to not wear gang clothing, and to not participate in gang activity. By Thanksgiving, 875 had reached their goals and their families received packaged holiday meals, which included turkeys and side dishes donated by a grocery chain.[124]

One student named "Ricky" said that at age 13, he was almost kicked out of school and was involved in a local gang. But an intervention meeting with OCGRIP called by his school's principal became a landmark event in his life.[125]

"All the negative stuff I took out of my life and they actually opened doors and explained to me what was going to happen if I kept on the same path ... it was pretty scary," he said.[126]

Ricky eventually graduated from high school, the *Register* reported in the fall of 2017, and "is working full time and attending community college, with the goal of becoming a physical therapist."[127]

Students who meet OCGRIP's challenges are rewarded in other ways. The Los Angeles Angels, a program partner, have provided free tickets to students and then given them special treatment and recognition at games. The Orange County Blues FC of the

> **They were challenged by OCGRIP to improve their school attendance, to avoid behavior that would result in disciplinary action, to not wear gang clothing, and to not participate in gang activity.**

United Soccer League hosted a camp where kids learned more about the sport, but also interacted with law enforcement officers. The hope is the participants, fourth-through eighth-graders, would "remember these moments and choose right from wrong," according to Danny Arreguin, a deputy probation officer who works in the gang unit of Orange County probation office, and also coaches socceer.[128]

OCGRIP also conducts curfew sweeps—in which minors unaccompanied after hours are detained, taken away for processing, then picked up by parents—organizes mentor programs, and performs truancy sweeps.[129]

Chapter 5
Not So-Safe Learning Environments: Rising Violence in California Schools

There have been many instances of appalling crimes on school campuses, ranging from peer-to-peer bullying to classroom sexual assaults that make every parent shudder with fear for the safety of their own children.
– Lance Izumi, ***The Corrupt Classroom***

Public schools are not only often failing students and parents academically, they are failing them in non-academic ways, too. Research by Lance Izumi, senior director of the Center for Education at the Pacific Research Institute, shows that classrooms have become unsafe environments. He's not referring specifically to school shootings, which according to research are actually "extraordinarily rare,"[130, 131, 132] but violence committed by students on teachers and fellow students that disrupts academic instruction and leaves behind battered victims.

Classrooms should be safe spaces. In its 2017 Indicators of School Crime and Safety, released in March 2018, the National Center for Education Statistics said, "Our nation's schools should be safe havens for teaching and learning, free of crime and violence. Any instance of crime or violence at school not only affects the individuals involved, but also may disrupt the educational process and affect bystanders, the school itself, and the surrounding community."[133]

Nationally, violent crime in the classroom has been falling. The 2016 NCES report said that, "During the 2013–14 school year, 65 percent of public schools recorded that one or more incidents of violence had taken place, amounting to an estimated 757,000 crimes," a rate of roughly 15 crimes per 1,000 students enrolled.[134] A year later, the NCES reported:

During the 2015–16 school year, 79 percent of public schools recorded that one or more incidents of violence, theft, or other crimes had taken place, amounting to 1.4 million. This translates to a rate of 28 crimes per 1,000 students enrolled in 2015–16. During the same school year, 47 percent of schools reported one or more of the specified crimes to the police, amounting to 449,000 crimes, or 9 crimes per 1,000 students enrolled.[135]

According to the 2014 report, "During the 2009–10 school year, 85 percent of public schools recorded that one or more crime incidents had taken place at school, amounting to an estimated 1.9 million crimes," which is a rate of 40 crimes per 1,000 public school students enrolled.[136] The respective numbers for the 2007-08 academic year were 85 percent, 2 million crimes, and 43 crimes per 100,000.[137]

In 2013-14, roughly 58 percent of public schools recorded one or more incidents of a physical attack or fight where no weapon was involved, 47 percent recorded one or more incidents of a threat of a physical attack without a weapon, and 13 percent recorded one or more serious violent incidents.[138] The 2009-10 data show 74 percent of public schools recording one or more violent incidents of crime, and 16 percent recording one or more serious violent incidents.[139] Two years earlier, 75 percent of public schools recorded one or more violent incidents of crime and 17 percent recorded one or more serious violent incidents.[140]

TABLE 2: PERCENTAGE OF CALIFORNIA PUBLIC SCHOOL TEACHERS WHO REPORTED BEING THREATENED WITH INJURY OR PHYSICALLY ATTACKED BY A STUDENT, 1993–94 THROUGH 2011–12

	THREATENED WITH INJURY	PHYSICALLY ATTACKED
1993-94	7.4	2.9
1999-00	5.8	2.5
2003-04	6	2
2007-08	8.5	3.6
2011-12	7.7	4.4

Source: Indicators of School Crime and Safety 2016, National Center for Education Statistics, Table 5.2

Izumi says that the statistics, "if anything, understate the problem."

"There is a crime epidemic on school campuses," he said, but due to a reluctance to report crimes to police, it's not showing up in the data as strongly as it should. Parents should "be more worried" than they are if they're basing their concerns solely on the data.[141]

Roy Verduzco, a teacher at Bullard High School in Fresno, was reportedly attacked by a sophomore female student in November 2015 when he tried to intervene in a fight between that student and another female student. Verduzco was hospitalized. It was the third incident of violence at the school during the academic year. School officials did not call 911 to report the assault, and the Bullard High School resource officer was not on campus when the incident occurred. The *Fresno Bee* reported that the alleged assailant was "taken to the office but was allowed to leave with her mother."[142]

In September 2015, a 15-year-old female student at Roosevelt High School in Fresno was charged with felony assault for punching a substitute teacher multiple times in the face, then following him out of the classroom. Apparently, the student refused to put up her cellphone when asked to by the teacher.[143] Two other 15-year-old female students at Roosevelt were also arrested in September 2015 for beating a third girl.[144]

A May 2016 campus brawl at Sylmar High School went on for 20 minutes and involved up to 40 students. A dozen officers were needed to break it up.[145]

Acts of violence often go unpunished. This is not due to administrative mistakes but a policy goal of cutting suspensions.

"Trash talk" on social media was reportedly the reason behind the attack of one Simi Valley High School by two students who lured him out of class. The victim was bruised on the left side of his head and had a tooth loosened after being sucker-punched.[146]

Acts of violence often go unpunished. This is not due to administrative mistakes but a policy goal of cutting suspensions. *Investor's Business Daily* published an editorial in 2014 headlined "Thugs Run L.A. Classrooms, Thanks To Obama Suspension Plan," which quoted teachers from the Los Angeles Unified School District who witnessed the threats and violence. One claimed to have been "terrified and bullied by a fourth-grade student," while another said, "this year at my high school we saw a far higher number of students acting as if they were running the campus and acting as they were on the same level as the teacher."[147] The teachers blamed a policy that replaced suspensions and other punishments with "restorative justice therapy."

The San Francisco Unified School District adopted its "Safe and Supportive Schools Policy" in 2014 which requires teachers to exhaust all options and resources before the student is kicked out of school or even sent to the principal's office. Within two years, frustrated parents were demonstrating in support of elementary school teacher Erika Keil, who spoke against the district policy but was reportedly ignored by the school administration. One of the parents demonstrating, Louella Hill, pointed out how dangerous schools have become. "Students have been choked, they've been slapped, they have been given death threats almost daily," she said.[148]

The Pasadena Unified School Board is another that has decided that students who engaged in "willful defiance," which includes such acts as using a cell phone in class, violating the dress code, and swearing at and defying teachers, and other disruptive behavior, would no longer be expelled or suspended.[149]

Oakland schools have, as well, eliminated willful defiance as grounds for suspension for students in grades four through 12. The Oakland Unified school board voted unanimously in 2015 to end the practice, and at the same time, the board voted to spend $2.3 million to expand its restorative justice program.[150]

The California Legislature and then-Governor Jerry Brown took the willful defiance policy statewide in 2015 but limited it to students in grades kindergarten through three. That law expired on July 1, 2018, and legislation to extend the policy to all students K-12 was vetoed by Brown in September 2018.[151] Without the veto, California would have become the only state to have extended the leniency to all students.[152]

Izumi points out that, "despite the lack of rigorous research showing that restorative justice is effective in changing student behavior for the better, 27 states have enacted laws that have limited the use of suspensions and other so-called 'exclusionary discipline policies.' "[153]

Then there's "the extreme" example from the Los Angeles Unified School District, which "has virtually banned suspensions, with the rate falling to near zero percent."[154]

> Criminal behavior and other discipline-related disruptions in the classroom not only increase risk for bodily injury and financial loss, but when transgressions go unpunished, including those that don't reach the level of criminal behavior, academics suffer.

Do these anti-suspension policies work? Research from the University of Chicago shows that when school officials in Chicago required "school leaders ask permission from the district office for long-term suspensions for nonviolent misbehavior," "teachers reported more disruptive classrooms and students reported less peer respect," writes Max Eden, a Manhattan Institute senior fellow.[155]

> After New York made principals ask permission for short-term suspensions for nonviolent misbehavior, I documented that, at half of all schools surveyed, students reported more frequent physical fighting and lower levels of peer respect, with the worst effects felt in schools serving 90-plus percent minority students.[156]
>
> And after Los Angeles eliminated suspensions for nonviolent 'willful defiance,' the portion of students who said they felt safe in their school plummeted from 72 percent to 60 percent.[157]

An examination of the School District of Philadelphia's policy to ban out-of-school suspensions for "low level" offenses found that the changes "were associated with improved attendance – but not improved achievement – for previously suspended students," while "'Never-suspended' peers (i.e., students who didn't receive a suspension in any of the years considered by the study) experienced worse outcomes in the most economically and academically disadvantaged schools, which were also the schools that did not (or could not) comply with the ban on conduct suspensions."[158]

David Griffith, a senior research and policy associate at the Thomas B. Fordham Institute, indicates that the casualties of anti-suspension policies are the large numbers of students who are not causing problems in schools.

> Overall, we agree that suspensions are unlikely to benefit suspended students. But an important question about school discipline is also whether the push to reduce the number of suspensions is harmful to the rule-abiding majority. According to a 2004 study, 85 percent of teachers and 73 percent of parents felt the 'school experience of most students suffers at the expense of a few chronic offenders.' And that was *before* the push to reduce suspensions.[159]

Criminal behavior and other discipline-related disruptions in the classroom not only increase risk for bodily injury and financial loss, but when transgressions go unpunished, including those that don't reach the level of criminal behavior, academics suffer. "There is evidence that disruptive students left in the classroom have a negative impact on the learning of their fellow students," writes Izumi,[160] who points out a University of California at Davis-University of Pittsburgh study which indicated "that troubled students have a statistically significant negative effect on their peer's reading and math test scores."[161]

"Adding one troubled student to a classroom of 20 students results in a decrease in student reading and math scores of more than two-thirds of a percentile point (2 to 3 percent of a standard deviation", according to EducationNext).[162] "In addition," Izumi writes, "a single disruptive student" significantly increases disruptive behavior in other students, "causing them to commit 16 percent more infractions than they would have otherwise."[163] He continues:

> If a disruptive student can have such a negative impact on his or her classmates, then the question is whether anti-suspension policies increase the level of classroom disruption, and, therefore, negatively impact non-disruptive students.[164]

When suspensions are removed, Izumi said, "you're going to get more of that behavior."[165]

"It's more dangerous to be in California schools than when we had zero-tolerance-type policies."[166]

Chapter 6
The Costs of Crime

Crime doesn't pay, supposedly. But it does cost society something.
The question is how much.
– Annie Lowrey, *Slate*, October 21, 2010

The financial losses incurred by victims are the most outward signs of the economic damage caused by crime. Property is damaged and stolen, lives are damaged and lost, and resources are spent on security. Some losses, however, are not as apparent. Criminal activity negatively affects incomes, property values, tourism revenue, and labor force participation. There are psychological effects, and loss of productivity and community spaces. Researchers Claudio Detotto and Edoardo Otranto say that criminal activity "acts like a tax on the entire economy." Moreover, "it discourages domestic and foreign direct investments, it reduces firms' competitiveness, and reallocates resources creating uncertainty and inefficiency."[167]

There is no single method for estimating the economic costs of crime. In attempting to determine the damage, the Rand Corporation averaged "recent studies that use three different approaches." The results indicate that each murder costs a little more than $9 million, while the cost of rape is $228,572 per incident. Aggravated assaults cost $91,694 each, robberies $70,641, burglaries $13,751, auto thefts $9,533, and larcenies $2,246.[168]

The cost of crime as a portion of economic output is 3.1 percent in localities served by the Los Angeles Police Department and 1.5 percent in localities served by the Los Angeles County Sheriff's Department. The figures are not out of line with other large cities. The cost of crime as a percent of economic output is 5.7 percent in Chicago, 4.8 percent in Dallas, 4.2 percent in Houston, and 1.6 in Miami-Dade County.[169]

Hiring additional law enforcement officers can mean significant economic benefits. Rand says its calculations "suggest that police personnel investments have substantial social returns." For each additional officer hired by the Los Angeles Police Department, the benefit is $482,966. The benefit is $151,369 for the Los Angeles County Sheriff's Department.

BENEFITS BY CITY FROM HIRING ADDITIONAL LAW ENFORCEMENT PERSONNEL (PER HIRE):

Houston	$797,819
Dallas	$673,316
Chicago	$391,655
Miami-Dade County	$304,561

Source: Rand Corporation

Some costs, says Rand, "such as fear of crime in general or loss of use of community spaces because of crime" "are difficult to objectively quantify." It's possible that "the intangible costs of crime may be substantially larger than the tangible costs."

While assigning costs to the loss of public spaces due to criminal activity might be elusive, the costs nevertheless exist. In September 2015, for instance, the city of San Diego closed the Dunes Park parking lot on Seacoast Drive due to criminal activity.[170] In the mid-1990s, Perry Park in Redondo Beach was a place of "intimidation, gunfire, drug dealing, and drunken gatherings at all hours of the night" as it "was serving as an informal headquarters for the North Side Redondo (NSR) gang." An intensive law enforcement effort was required before the residents could "freely use the park for recreational activities."[171] A 2010 feature series published by the *Sacramento Bee* found that "crime is on the rise in California's state parks, up nearly threefold in the last decade. Even serious and violent crimes were on the upswing." One of the consequences of the increased crime was "visitors spending less time in state parks for the first time in at least a decade, bucking a national trend."[172]

SOCIAL AND PERSONAL

In the summer of 2005, San Leandro Police Officer Nels "Dan" Niemi answered a disturbance call. Irving Alexander Ramirez was convicted of killing Niemi, shooting him ten times because he didn't want to be arrested for a parole violation.[173] Ramirez was subsequently sentenced to death. Niemi's wife Dionne said that she "was as angry as I was grief-stricken. For a while, I really fell apart. I was depressed and neglected the needs of my children."[174]

A female victim from Sacramento whose name was withheld in a University of California report said she is troubled by terrifying dreams. "If they're not nightmares," she said, "I sit and think about [what happened] every single day, every night before I go to sleep. I try everything, I tried to get high, drunk, just to forget about it, but it's there all the time. . . . The pain is there." An unnamed female from Stockton said that after being a victim, "some people feel worthless, and like, oh, it just happened to me. It's been happening to me. This is what I deserve. So who cares about it, and why should I have a voice and speak up?"[175]

Jens Ludwig of the University of Chicago wrote in 2010 that "the social costs of crime are so large that American society seems likely to be underinvesting right now in most forms of crime prevention, except for mass incarceration."[176]

The very fear of criminal activity in high-crime areas results in "economic and social effects" that "can span out into the surrounding city," according to the *Crime and Punishment in America Reference Library*.

"Residents become more withdrawn and defensive and less committed to their communities. The very social fiber of the community is weakened. Some communities adopt neighborhood watch programs to revitalize the community or avoid its decay."[177]

> **The social and personal effects of criminal activity include pain, suffering, and a diminished quality of life.**

The social and personal effects of criminal activity include pain, suffering, and a diminished quality of life. Friendships and family life are often disrupted. Victim-support groups say that those affected by crime sometimes develop long-term problems. Those can include depression, anxiety and even post-traumatic stress disorder.

Criminal activity also negatively impacts future economic prospects. One study found "that the economic chances of low-income kids, those who grow up at the bottom fifth of the economic ladder, are the most severely affected by violent crime. But those kids are also the ones who benefit most from a decline in violent crime in their neighborhoods."[178]

An effective path to decreasing crime in these neighborhoods is gentrification, which the Centers for Disease Control and Prevention defines "as the transformation of neighborhoods from low value to high value", though it "has the potential to cause displacement of long-time residents and businesses."[179] Gentrification is often criticized because of that displacement.

But those who remain, and those who are part of the influx, are safer. A Massachusetts Institute of Technology study concluded that gentrification in Cambridge, Mass., led to a 16 percent decrease in crime – and economic gains for the city, as well. Researchers found that the "reduction in violent crimes, specifically, resulted in the largest economic gains.".[180]

Apparently, gentrification scatters the criminals who previously preyed on the residents.

"According to the police, most of the people who commit crimes in Cambridge don't live there, so it is probably not simply a story that criminals were priced out and moved away," said Christopher Palmer, one of the report's authors. "There is evidence in the criminology and economics literatures that sometimes, when you disrupt violent social networks, crime declines in aggregate."[181]

In many cases, the social and personal impacts of crime are seen in the production of even greater criminal activity, since the behavior is often learned and reinforced. "Persistent exposure to adverse conditions such as community crime" is one factor in the promotion of "a hostile view of people and relationships, a preference for immediate rewards, and a cynical view of conventional norms," according to a criminology paper written by university sociologists Ronald L. Simons and Callie Harbin Burt.[182]

Chapter 7
Tipping the Scales of Justice:
A Review of California Crime Policy
and Reform Recommendations

The war on crime is a never-ending one. And it is necessary that we pursue it constantly and with vigor if our citizens are to be safe on our streets and in their homes, and if man is to be able to live free from fear of his fellow man in an ever-contracting world and an increasingly more complex society.
– Governor Ronald Reagan, April 1967

GUN LAWS

It's widely acknowledged that California has some of the strictest, if not the strictest, gun laws in the country. The Giffords Law Center to Prevent Gun Violence ranked California no. 1 in 2017[183] for the fifth-straight year for its restrictive firearm ownership policies. The Cato Institute ranks Hawaii as the only state with tougher laws, while Everytown ranks four states with a more rigorous regime.[184] Even with the reputation in place, lawmakers added more than a dozen new laws during the 2017-18 legislative session generally making it more difficult to own firearms.

Despite the smothering laws, the state ranked 14th in gun violence – 3.4 crimes per 100,000 residents from 2012 to 2016, according to DemographicData.org, which obtains its data from public sources. [185] Homicide crimes by firearms – not including non-criminal homicides – grew from 1,226 (70.1 percent of all criminal homicides in 2011) to 1,368 (71.9 percent of all criminal homicides) in 2016,[186] then fell in 2018 to 1,274 (70.9 percent).[187] The lowest figure over the intervening years was 1,169 (70.4 percent) in 2014.[188]

Aggravated assaults by firearm and robberies in which firearms have been used have also increased in some of the state's biggest cities in recent years.

TABLE 3: AGGRAVATED ASSAULTS BY FIREARMS

The pendulum has been swinging back toward more incidents of aggravated assault and robberies with firearms after several years of decreases in California's biggest cities, with the exception of Oakland.

	LOS ANGELES	SAN DIEGO	SAN FRANCISCO	SAN JOSE	OAKLAND
2007	4,546	689	278	305	1,208
2008	3,552	542	255	265	1,386
2009	3,283	437	212	242	1,067
2010	3,156	402	248	238	1,196
2011	2,933	318	227	272	1,410
2012	2,679	434	178	408	1,598
2013	2,325	388	163	392	1,111
2014	2,506	349	378	367	1,310
2015	3,524	400	264	360	802
2016	4,243	461	310	431	817
2017	4,068	364	295	507	592

Source: Open Justice, California Department of Justice, Data Exploration, Crime Statistics, Crimes and Clearances

TABLE 4: ROBBERIES WITH FIREARMS

	LOS ANGELES	SAN DIEGO	SAN FRANCISCO	SAN JOSE	OAKLAND
2007	4,909	448	905	215	1,787
2008	4,437	393	1,030	220	1,810
2009	4,088	375	817	197	1,471
2010	3,577	321	763	214	1,615
2011	2,887	276	617	251	1,927
2012	2,363	284	705	336	2,553
2013	2,220	239	840	293	3,140
2014	2,042	219	676	282	1,861
2015	2,294	185	616	298	1,755
2016	2,816	239	563	281	1,552
2017	2,804	220	576	381	1,202

Source: Open Justice, California Department of Justice, Data Exploration, Crime Statistics, Crimes and Clearances

While gun ownership rights are among the weakest in the country, California has been been slow to keep firearms out of the hands of those who have been prohibited by law from owning them. These individuals include convicted felons, persons with a history of violence or severe mental illness and wanted individuals.

The Armed and Prohibited Persons System was established in 2001 by Senate Bill 950 to keep guns from falling into the wrong hands. The APPS program "cross-references five databases to find people who legally purchased handguns and registered assault weapons since 1996 with those prohibited from owning or possessing a firearm," according to the office of the California attorney general. It is the first and only "automated system for tracking firearm owners who might fall into a prohibited status," in the country.[189] The state attorney general's office called the program "a highly sophisticated investigative tool that provides law enforcement agencies with information about gun owners who are legally prohibited from possessing firearms."[190]

While gun ownership rights are among the weakest in the country, California has been been slow to keep firearms out of the hands of those who have been prohibited by law from owning them.

Yet by January 2018, more than 10,000 "people remain(ed) on a list of Californians who legally purchased guns but were later disqualified from possessing them".[191]

California State Senate Republicans have complained about "the program's persistent backlog of unresolved cases."[192] "Despite DOJ's commitment in 2013 to eliminate the backlog (which peaked at just over 20,000 in 2014) within one year and having been provided nearly $68 million since then to do so, the attorney general recently reported that more than 10,000 prohibited individuals may still have their guns," according to the April 2018 Republican analysis.[193]

> California State Senate Republicans have complained about "the program's persistent backlog of unresolved cases."

"Although the Attorney General insisted the program is a high priority, the results are not impressive. The annual backlog reduction has declined from almost 4,800 cases cleared in 2015 to about 2,000 in 2016 (under the previous Attorney General), to just 408 in 2017. When asked to explain the slowdown, the department administrator stated, 'Back then, it was all hands on deck,' which seems to imply that the department no longer perceives a sense of urgency under the new Attorney General Xavier Becerra."[194]

A March 2018 report from the attorney general's office said it continues to run into "difficulty in filling special agent vacancies" for the program "due to factors outside of the Department's control, such as pay disparity with other state law enforcement agencies, attrition through retirements, and a change in retirement formulas that is unfavorable to new hires."[195]

Republicans have asked for an in-depth review of the APPS program, noting that "during testimony at a joint hearing of the Senate and Assembly Public Safety Committees about this backlog, the department's staff stated that 'in theory' they could eliminate the backlog in a very short time, perhaps even one year."[196]

They announced in April 2018 that given the attorney general's "dismal progress over the past year toward eliminating" the backlog, "we can only conclude that keeping firearms out of the hands of dangerous criminals and people with serious mental health issues is not a high priority for your office."[197]

"This sort of callous indifference all too often results in tragedy, followed by misplaced blame on guns rather than the criminals that abuse them," 13 GOP senators said in a letter to Becerra.[198]

While the state has been slow in keeping firearms out of the hands of those who shouldn't have them, it has also placed on the prohibited list the names of citizens who don't belong there. The state auditor's office has found that 37 percent of the names on the list shouldn't be on it. Second Amendment organizations say that figure is at least 40 percent and could be as high as 60 percent.[199] Either way, a lot of Californians are losing their firearms without a valid reason.

A 2016 media investigation reported that "after taking a closer look at the program, we found several mistakes that have been made along the way, as well as flaws that have been documented by state officials." Consider the "traumatizing" experience of Lynette Phillips, who "lives a quiet, ordinary life" in the "the quiet Southern California neighborhood of Upland," and whose tranquility was interrupted in 2013 "by a loud knock on the door" by police officers. They were looking for guns, Phillips said, of the "scary, embarrassing" event.[200]

"Phillips didn't know yet, but her name was listed in California's Armed and Prohibited Persons Systems. She was now considered someone who wasn't allowed to own, or be around, firearms. So, all of her husband's guns were confiscated, but not before being laid out on the front porch for neighbors to see."[201]

Phillips said she was the victim of "false documentation." While in a mental hospital to deal with an adverse reaction to changing anti-depressant drugs, a nurse considered her suicidal and entered it into her records. But Phillips says she didn't say what the nurse claimed she did. Phillips also voluntarily checked herself into the facility and the standard for seizing firearms under the APPS program is involuntary mental health commitments.[202]

"Although APPS is good in theory, in practice, its impact ranges from incidental to unjust," says *Ammoland*, a sport shooting publication. "Many, if not most, people on the prohibited list don't know it, aren't dangerous, and could have their gun rights restored by simply filing some paperwork."[203]

> While the state has been slow in keeping firearms out of the hands of those who shouldn't have them, it has also placed on the prohibited list the names of citizens who don't belong there.

REFORM RECOMMENDATIONS:
Follow the State Auditor's recommendations and fix the implementation of the APPS Program.

The idea that prompted lawmakers to enact the APPS program, which is unique to California, is noble. But implementation needs to be improved. Its resources need to be appropriately applied, the velocity in which its provisions are being fulfilled must accelerate, and its practice of capturing so many of the wrong people in its dragnet can't be allowed to continue.

While those matters are being attended to, freedom- and self-defense minded policymakers should pursue:

- An initiative that will establish in the California Constitution the right to bear arms so that the APPS program cannot be abused;

- A state "shall-issue" law so that law enforcement authorities cannot reject a citizen's permit application for arbitrary reasons; and

- Ensuring, through new policy if needed, that the names that wrongly appear on the prohibited list database can be promptly removed through an administrative petition.

Recidivism

California defines recidivism as "conviction of a new felony or misdemeanor committed within three years of release from custody or committed within three years of placement on supervision for a previous criminal conviction." This changed in 2013 with the enactment of Assembly Bill 1050. Previously, recidivism was measured by a return to prison rather than a conviction.[204]

The narrower definition hides the fact that while released inmates continue to offend, they are not being incarcerated at the same rate. Since 2002-03, the conviction rate for previously convicted persons has remained steady, from 47.7 percent to 46.1 percent in 2012-13, the most recent year for which data are available. The return-to-prison rate, however, has fallen from 66.2 percent to 22.2 percent over the same period.[205]

When the state embarked on its "realignment" program to meet a federal court order that mandated a reduction in the prison population, there was concern that it would increase recidivism. At that time – 2011 – California had the highest recidivism rate in the country. Roughly seven of every 10 inmates went back to prison after committing a crime post-release.[206] Veteran columnist Dan Walters wrote that there is "continuing controversy over whether the realigned felons who otherwise might be in prison are committing new crimes in serious numbers."[207]

Some have argued that California has not done enough to rehabilitate inmates and focused too much on building additional prison units, a mistake that has produced the high recidivism rate. But it appears to be more of a case of a failure of implementation than a lack of attention. The Legislative Analyst's Office says that "various rehabilitation programs . . . have several shortcomings."

"Based on our review of the (California Department of Corrections and Rehabilitation's) inprison rehabilitation programs, we conclude that they have several shortcomings," says the LAO. "This is because CDCR (1) often falls short in adhering to . . . three key principles (programs must be evidence-based, cost-effective, and focused on highest-risk, highest-need inmates) for reducing recidivism, (2) does not effectively use all of its rehabilitation program slots despite waitlists for such programs, and (3) has a flawed approach to measuring program performance, which makes it difficult to determine whether existing program resources are being used effectively."[208]

The LAO says the state's rehabilitation programs would be more successful if:

- Lawmakers required programs to be evidence based.
- Officials measured the actual cost-effectiveness of the programs.
- Programs were more effectively targeted toward the highest risk and highest need inmates.
- Existing rehabilitation resources were more efficiently used.
- Performance measures were improved so that regular oversight is enabled.[209]

"We recommend the Legislature take various steps to improve CDCRs inprison rehabilitation programs to maximize recidivism reduction, which would in turn reduce the number of victims in the future and result in state and local fiscal benefits."[210]

REFORM RECOMMENDATIONS:
Embrace non-profit, private-sector, and public-private-partnership rehabilitation programs

There are private-sector alternatives to government rehabilitation programs. Outside organizations, which are generally referred to as Inmate Leisure Time Activity Groups, says the LAO, "are groups initiated by inmates and volunteers that provide various rehabilitation opportunities – such as self-help support, creative writing, or peer mentorship."

"These programs allow inmates to be engaged in activities outside state-funded rehabilitation programs and/or work assignments. (Work assignments allow inmates to earn wages for jobs they perform within prisons, such as janitorial work or cooking meals.) Some of the programs require inmates to complete a specific rehabilitative curriculum, such as a one-year long violence prevention and life skills program. Other programs have a less clearly defined curriculum, such as the various self-help support groups in prisons."[211]

There is also the California Prison Industry Authority (CalPIA) "a semiautonomous state agency that provides work assignments and vocational training (like certain Career Technical Education rehabilitation programs) to inmates. It is funded primarily through the sale of the goods and services produced by the program. California law requires state agencies to purchase products and services offered by CalPIA whenever possible."[212]

The centerpiece of CalPIA is its Career Technical Education program, which teaches carpentry, iron-work, commercial diving, computer-aided design, and construction labor skills. Also, under the CTE umbrella is Code.7370. Operated in a partnership with San Francisco-based prison rehabilitation nonprofit The Last Mile, and supervised by CalPIA instructors, Code.7370 teaches inmates computer coding and web design, and trains them in HTML, JavaScript, CSS, and Python.

Chris Schuhmacher, who served 17 years at San Quentin, was one of the early Code.7370 graduates. When he first arrived in the class, he said, "I was at ground zero. But, I had a willingness to learn." His biggest fear, he added, "was what type of life I would have upon my release." But now, "thanks to Code.7370, I have the answer."[213]

Schuhmacher completed hundreds of hours of training during the six-month class. Those "679 hours have changed the trajectory of my life," he said. "It has inspired me to want to pay this gift forward. Upon my release I'd like to donate 679 hours of my time to give others the opportunity to learn what I've learned."[214]

Shortly after being released on parole in 2017, Schuhmacher was blending "in with the Silicon Valley crowd as a software engineering intern at a bustling tech firm, ditching his blue prison uniform for a sweater and khakis, and his cell for a cubicle." As of May 2018, Schuhmacher was working at Fandom, described as "an entertainment site where super-fans can read and post content on everything from 'Game of Thrones' to 'Pokémon.'"[215]

Another graduate of that first class, Aly Tamboura, has also been released on parole. He was hired by Facebook cofounder, chairman and CEO Mark Zuckerberg.[216] All told, more than a dozen inmates have graduated from the program and have gone on to jobs on the outside.[217]

A fully private organization that operates outside of prison walls that has garnered praise for its work is Homeboy Industries, which opened its first Homeboy Bakery in 1992 in Los Angeles. It has been called "the largest gang intervention and rehabilitation program in the world,"[218] and won a Bon Appétit Award in the humanitarian category in 2007.[219] Homeboy founder Rev. Gregory J. Boyle received the 2017 Laetare Medal from the University of Notre Dame for serving "men and women who have been incarcerated and involved with gangs, and, in doing so, has helped them to discover the strength and hope necessary to transform their lives."[220]

> There are private-sector alternatives to government rehabilitation programs.

Will Lopez, a one-time gang member, first incarcerated as a 15-year-old, then released from prison when he was 23, is a product of the Homeboy process. "I wasn't ready to change," after being released, Lopez said. "If anything, I thought I got slicker, smarter and wiser through those years. I moved out of my neighborhood, but my neighborhood was still in me. I kept going in and out of jail for parole violations."[221]

After many attempts by Boyle to reach Lopez, he finally "walked in the doors of Homeboy Industries," and since has never looked back. "I fell in love with the place, and the place fell in love with me. I'm a completely different person now—supporting my daughter through daycare, a loyal husband to my wife, a student . . . I wear a lot of hats."[222]

> My life is good today, and I can do the things I never imagined – have a job, be a good father, go to the beach. And it's all thanks to this program. Homeboy teaches me life skills, it teaches me to treat people differently, to treat myself differently, to accept who I was in the past and who I am today.[223]

Jose Osuna entered the Homeboy program in 2009. He had been a gang member for 25 years, in prison for 13. "When I decided to change my life, I was so grateful that there was a place for me, and there was a man named Gregory Boyle," Osuna said.

"After completing the core program at Homeboy, Osuna became a student in the solar panel training and certification program and was then promoted to serve as the program's leader," *National Jesuit News* reported. "After three years, he assumed the role of director of employment services for two years. He has now spent the past two years in his current position as director of external affairs" for Homeboy Industries.[224]

"I probably wouldn't get anywhere outside of Homeboy. And that's my reality," Osuna says.[225]

Other social enterprises under the Homeboy Industries umbrella include Homegirl Café, Homeboy Gear, Homeboy Diner, catering services, grocery products, and farmers markets stands.

Another route to improved rehabilitation is the pressure government can apply to privately owned prisons by tying contract payments to the recidivism rates of inmates formerly housed in those facilities. (There are roughly 2,000 inmates being housed in private prisons in California.) Private prisons that turn out the best-behaved parolees and released felons are rewarded financially. After Pennsylvania rebid its contracts with private prisons in 2013 and tied compensation to the prison operators in the new contracts to their reductions in recidivism rates, recidivism from those facilities fell 11 percent between July 2014 and June 2015.[226]

Three Strikes Law

The Legislature passed a law in 1994, which was also supported by voters when they approved Proposition 184, requiring defendants who have a prior felony conviction and are later convicted for another felony to be sentenced to twice the term that is mandated for the crime. Defendants with two or more prior felony convictions were sentenced to 25 years to life for an additional felony conviction.[227]

Voters amended the Three Strikes Law in 2012 with Proposition 36, which required the third strike to be a serious or violent felony for it to qualify as a 25 years-to-life sentence. It further allowed inmates who are serving a third-strike sentence to ask the court to reduce that sentence if they would have been eligible for a second-strike sentence under the reform.[228]

In 2017, the California Supreme Court ruled 4-3 that judges have wide latitude in refusing to shorten sentences of inmates who petition the courts under Proposition 36.[229]

A little more than one-third of the state's inmate population is made up of second- and third-strikers.[230] This would seem to indicate that the law has worked as designed – to keep habitual offenders off the streets and out of communities.

A report from a trio of university scholars found that "three states (California, Louisiana, and New Jersey) showed a statistically significant decrease in four or more crime categories," after three-strikes implementation, "but a statistically significant increase in at least one crime category as well."[231]

But the authors were not prepared to credit the state's Three Strikes Law for the reduction. "While it would be tempting to conclude that three strikes laws are responsible for the majority of the crime drop in these states, especially in California, where three-strike provisions are applied quite frequently, one must account for the fact that the results for some laws are probably nothing more than random artifacts or are proxies for other contemporaneous changes taking place around the adoption of a three strikes law, not explicitly controlled for in the model specifications."[232]

But this conclusion does not appear to be a definitive rejection of Three Strikes as an effective deterrent to crime. Nor does it seem to be an endorsement of further reform of the law.

Voters amended the Three Strikes Law in 2012 with Proposition 36, which required the third strike to be a serious or violent felony for it to qualify as a 25 years-to-life sentence.

REFORM RECOMMENDATIONS:

When voters passed Proposition 184 by a 72-28 margin, they were likely thinking, as Fresno County Assistant District Attorney Steve Wright has said, that the "law is in place for a reason – to make sure that individuals . . . are held accountable for their crimes and that the public is kept safe."[233]

For example, a proposed California state ballot initiative (which failed to make the 2018 ballot) would have exempted burglaries and robberies without physical harm from the Three Strikes law.[234] The initiative gets it about half right. Most would likely agree that sending a burglar who stole from an unoccupied home to prison for life is not necessarily justice. But robbery is different. The absence of physical harm during a robbery doesn't lessen its seriousness. Even when there is no bodily injury, robbery victims' lives are threatened because violence is implied.

California's Three Strikes law should continue to severely punish violent offenders. But those who commit what are considered serious but not violent crimes should not be caught in the 25-years-to-life dragnet. Any further reform of the law needs to better define the offenses that constitute third strikes, limiting them to actual, serious felonies that either cause or imply bodily harm.

Public Safety Realignment

Over a three-day period in March 2013 there were 11 shootings in Southern California. The incidents included a shooting in Downey, where the suspect shot two people in a restaurant parking lot; a man shot and killed as he walked the streets of Panorama City; and a person critically wounded in the Los Angeles neighborhood of Echo Park. Covina Police Chief Kim Raney said he believed that the series of shootings was in part due to a policy called "realignment."[235]

On Christmas Day 2012, 49-year-old Victor McClinton of Pasadena, a community volunteer was killed by a stray shot from a nearby gang-related shooting. Larry Darnell Bishop, then a 20-year-old "reputed gang member" from Chino was arrested. Bishop "had been released early from county jail without supervision, where he was serving time for a felony assault with a deadly weapon conviction under the state's prison realignment program." He was eventually sentenced to life in prison.[236]

> In 2006, California's prison population reached an all-time high of nearly 163,000 more than double the system's design capacity of 80,000.

In 2006, California's prison population reached an all-time high of nearly 163,000,[237] more than double the system's design capacity of 80,000.[238] The *Economist* called California prisons "gulags in the sun" in 2009 and reflected on the two-day August riot at Chino in which inmates "smashed glass to use the shards as knives and ripped off pipes for bludgeons," while "burning down part of the prison and injuring hundreds." The magazine implied that the riot was caused by the "overcrowding that plagues California's 33 prisons as a whole" and predicted that it would not "be the last in California's dreadful prison system."[239]

That same year, then-Gov. Arnold Schwarzenegger said state prisons were "dangerously overcrowded," had reached a "crisis point," and insisted that "swift and dramatic action" was needed to keep the state prison system falling under federal control.[240]

Five years later, the state began moving tens of thousands of inmates from state prisons to county jails, and in some cases back into the streets through early release. The program was authorized by Assembly Bills 109 and 117 of that year, which were passed with only Democrats voting for them. Then-Gov. Jerry Brown signed them both and re-alignment began on Oct. 1. The bills were in response to a May 2011 U.S. Supreme Court ruling that upheld the 2009 order of a three-judge panel, which said the state prisons were overcrowded and could not house more than 137.5 percent of the state facilities' design capacity of about 79,000. Consequently, California prisons could not hold more than 109,805 inmates at any given time. To satisfy the court order, the state had to reduce the prison population by 34,433 inmates by June 27, 2013.[241]

The prison population fell sharply almost immediately – 27,000 inmates were transferred out of state prisons in the first year.[242] By 2018, the inmate population was still 127,400,[243] which included 4,300 inmates housed in two out-of-state privately run prisons, and another 4,100 in private facilities in California.[244] (It is also worth noting that realignment supporters promised that it would save taxpayers money. That hasn't happened. The 2018-19 Department of Corrections and Rehabilitation budget is $12.1 billion.[245] The budget for the 2007-08 fiscal year, the year after the prison population peaked, was $10.1 billion.[246])

Realignment "was premised on the idea that locals can do a better job, and it was hoped that incarceration rates and corrections costs would fall," notes the Public Policy Institute of California.[247] Linda Penner, chair of the California Board of Community Corrections, said that before the program was established, "we were spending a great deal of money on incarceration and we weren't getting good outcomes."[248]

Inmates to be transferred were "certain low-level offenders, parole violators, and parolees" who were the state's responsibility. Their offenses were to be limited to "non-violent, non-serious, and non-sex."[249] Yet some of the "realigned" inmates were found guilty of serious crimes. In 2011, the Associated Press "revealed that crimes that qualify for local sentences include at least two dozen offenses that can be considered serious or violent."[250]

Among them: Involuntary manslaughter, vehicular manslaughter while intoxicated, killing or injuring a police officer while resisting arrest, participating in a lynching, possession of weapons of mass destruction, possessing explosives, threatening a witness or juror, and using arson or explosives to terrorize a health facility or church. Assault, battery, statutory rape and sexual exploitation by doctors or psychotherapists are also covered by the prison realignment law and carry sentences that will be served in a county jail instead of state prison.[251]

An August 2011 report from the Public Policy Institute of California noted the concerns about "the concept of 'nonserious' crimes that are nevertheless felonies."

"These crimes include a variety of offenses that would strike many civilians as far from trivial. . . . Among the offenses no longer making the nonserious list are 'assault resulting in death of a child under eight,' 'unlawfully causing a fire that causes an inhabited structure to burn,' and 'solicitation for murder.'"[252]

Several weeks before the "the biggest criminal justice experiment ever conducted in America"[253] began, the California Department of Justice released its annual crime report, which indicated that crime rates had been falling. Highlights from the report:

- From 2010 to 2011, the violent crime rate per 100,000 population decreased 2.1 percent (from 422.3 to 413.3), reaching its lowest level since 1968 (411.1).

- The number of homicide crimes continued to decline in 2011. Since peaking in 1993, the number of homicide crimes has decreased 56.2 percent (from 4,095 to 1,794).

- The aggravated assault rate has declined steadily since peaking in 1992.

- The 2011 burglary rate of 612.9 per 100,000 population is one-half the 1966 rate of 1,225.9.

- Since peaking in 1989, the motor vehicle theft rate has decreased 62.3 percent.

- The arson rate per 100,000 population declined 43.7 percent from 2006 to 2011.[254]

In 2012, the rate of violent crimes rose to 424.7 per 100,000 and the rate of property crimes increased from 2,593.7 per 100,000 to 2,772.6. Rates for both fell over the next two years before rising in 2015. The violent crime rate increased again in 2017, while the property crime rate dropped.[255] The violent crime rate increased 12.5 percent from 2011, the year realignment was begun, to 2016, and 11.2 percent from 2012 to 2017[256] while property crime rates rose 2.7 percent from 2011 to 2016,[257] then fell 5.9 percent from 2012 to 2017.[258]

Were the increases in crime due to realignment? Or has the program successfully met its intended goals? The answers depend on who is responding.

"Is California more dangerous as a result of realignment? The answer is 'no,'" says Carroll Seron, a University of California, Irvine, criminology professor who co-guest edited a February 2016 issue of *The Annals of the American Academy of Political & Social Science* that was entirely dedicated to realignment.[259] Data have shown crime rising for the three years between 2015 and 2017.

Charis Kubrin, also a UCI criminology professor, said "There are so many factors in crime increases: poverty, gun availability, demographic shifts, drug markets, gang activity, I can go on and on."

Two researchers who contributed an article to the issue said they had found "very little evidence that the large reduction in California incarceration had an effect on violent crime, and modest evidence of effects on property crime, auto theft in particular." Magnus Lofstrum of the Public Policy Institute of California and University of California Berkeley public policy professor Steven Raphael also said the program had little effect on recidivism.[260]

Critics of realignment were concerned that realignment would increase crime. Given that only a portion of those "realigned" remain incarcerated in local jails – statewide the jail population increased by fewer than 9,000 in the first year of the program, "about one-third of the decline in the prison population," according to the Public Policy Institute of California[261] – their apprehensions appear valid. Several incidents have highlighted those concerns.

- "In June 2013, a few months after Dustin James Kinnear, 26, was released from prison and placed on community supervision under the realignment initiative, he stabbed to death a 23-year-old woman on the Hollywood Walk of Fame because she refused to give him a dollar," Bishop Noel Jones, pastor at City of Refuge in Gardena wrote in January 2018 in the *Los Angeles Sentinel*. "Ka Pasasouk shot and killed four people in Los Angeles County in December 2012 while on community supervision under the Realignment Act."[262]

- "Michael Christopher Mejia, 26, was arrested Monday after Whittier police Officer Keith Boyer was fatally shot and Officer Patrick Hazell was wounded as they responded to the site of a traffic accident Mejia was involved in," the Associated Press reported in February 2017. Though "a spokesman for the California Department of Corrections and Rehabilitation said none of the state's recent criminal justice reform initiatives affected the length of Mejia's prison sentence," "a local police union and two Los Angeles legislators have called for investigations into the policies surrounding Mejia's release."[263]

Authorities said Mejia was released from California's Pelican State Prison in April and was placed on probation under a reform measure known as Assembly Bill 109 that allowed some convicted felons to serve their sentences in county jails and serve probation instead of being sent to state prisons and paroled.[264]

- The shooting death of 52-year-old Sacramento County Sheriff's Deputy Robert French in August 2017 has also been blamed on realignment. Thomas Daniel Littlecloud, who died in the shootout in which two other officers were wounded, was the suspected shooter.[265]

  Prior to AB 109, a no bail warrant for a violation of parole would have been issued for Littlecloud and served upon him. He would have remained in custody while awaiting both resolution of his new criminal cases and a parole revocation hearing. Most importantly, he would not have been on the streets in August 2017 and able to murder Deputy French," the Association for Los Angeles Deputy Sheriffs said in a statement. "The attempt by the state legislator to game recidivism statistics doesn't change the reality of parolee behavior and law violations after release from prison.[266]

- Michael Rushford, president of the Criminal Justice League Foundation in Sacramento said in late 2017 that "Over the past 14 months, five California police officers have been killed by habitual criminals who would have been in jail or state prison prior to the 2011 enactment of AB109, Gov. Brown's 'Public Safety Realignment' law."[267]

Rushford said that "a study by the San Francisco-based anti-incarceration group Center on Juvenile and Criminal Justice" that has been used to show there has been no increase in crime in the state since the state adopted sentencing reforms in 2011 is "bogus."[268]

"The key to the study's findings is its lumping of violent and property crime into the category named 'overall crime.' By doing this, the increasing violent crime in California is offset by the decrease in property crime," he said, adding that property crime rates have fallen because some have been reclassified by misdemeanors by Proposition 47.[269]

"When the focus is on violent crimes in California, state and federal data indicate dramatic increases."[270]

REFORM RECOMMENDATIONS:
Increase use of out-of-state beds to house California inmates

The state cannot ignore the federal court order to cut its prison population, though given it has defied federal immigration law with its declared sanctuary state status, it seems state government has become selective about which federal rules it will comply with. Even so, realignment was not a necessary measure to ease California's prison overcrowding.

Rather than making sweeping changes to sentencing and parole policies, the state could have transferred prison inmates to other states that have the room to accommodate them. In addition to approving funding for more prison and jail space – some of which was later cancelled – 2007's Assembly Bill 900 authorized the temporary housing of as many as 8,000 inmates out-of-state while 40,000 new prison beds and 13,000 new jail beds were added. Four years later, as many as 10,000 California inmates were housed out of state. Yet rather than continue to use that avenue, the number housed out of state had fallen to 4,300 by the end of 2017.[271]

Housing inmates out of state is also fiscally responsible. The California Department of Finance estimated in 2014, when officials were facing an impending deadline to reduce prison populations, that the cost of sending an inmate to an out-of-state facility was $29,500 a year.[272] At that time, the cost of housing a prisoner for one year in California was $47,000.[273] The annual housing cost for an inmate in California today has grown to $75,560, the highest per-inmate cost in the country.[274]

Proposition 47

On Nov. 4, 2014, California voters approved Proposition 47 by nearly a 60-40 margin. It reduced "certain drug possession felonies to misdemeanors" and required "misdemeanor sentencing for petty theft, receiving stolen property, and forging/writing bad checks when the amount involved is $950 or less."[275]

The California Department of Corrections and Rehabilitation says that no inmate is automatically released from state prison due to Prop. 47, yet the "new law allows people who are already serving a felony conviction for these crimes to petition the court for resentencing." Prop. 47 also allows "a person who has completed his/her sentence for the specified offenses to file an application before the trial court to have the felony conviction reduced to a misdemeanor."[276] There are exceptions to who can petition the court. Those who have previous convictions for the following are not eligible to petition:[277]

- Sex offenders, including those convicted of rape
- Convicted child molesters
- Inmates registered as sex offenders
- Those convicted of murder and attempted murder
- Those convicted of solicitation to commit murder
- Those convicted of assault with a machine gun on an officer
- Those convicted of any serious or violent crime punishable by a life sentence or death

Under Prop. 47, penalties were reduced specifically for grand theft, shoplifting, receiving stolen goods, writing bad checks, check forgery, and drug possession for personal use. It was a profound change in how the state treated less-serious offenders.

Supporters said that rather than treat low-level crimes as rigorously as they had been, the criminal justice focus needed to shift toward rehabilitation, and "smart on crime" programs. They believed that funding for mental health care, education and treatment for offenders who had no business in prison needed to be increased.[278] Freeing up funds to apply to more serious and violent crimes – $103 million through the spring of 2017 – as well as lowering the state prison populations were also goals of Prop. 47.[279]

Some believe that the surge in automobile break-ins in San Francisco can be blamed on Prop. 47.

"People want their government to make a distinction in the public safety area between those who have to be locked up and those who can serve their sentence in less expensive, more humane and more effective ways," said former California Senate President Pro Tem and current Sacramento mayor Darrell Steinberg. "That's what the people want."[280]

But not everyone was optimistic.

"Proposition 47 will not eliminate crime; it has only reduced the consequences of crime," then-Sacramento County District Attorney Jan Scully said just after the 2014 elections. "When you reduce the consequences of crime, then there are some people who won't be deterred from committing crime."[281]

Since the passing of Prop. 47, some opponents have said that the ballot measure has left law enforcement with less incentive to pursue low-level offenders. "Even if the person is escorted to the station, odds are great he'll be back on the street in an hour or so," Erica Sandberg, a San Francisco journalist and community advocate wrote in *National Review* in 2018, more than three years after the measure had passed.[282]

Residents who are experiencing an uptick in so-called low-level crimes in their neighborhoods are baffled by studies indicating" that the law did not increase crime.

For example, a December 2017 Center on Criminal and Juvenile Justice report shows property crimes down by an average of 18.1 percent across the state. "Those numbers are false," says Michael Rushford, president of the Sacramento-based Criminal Justice Legal Foundation, a nonprofit public-interest law organization: "More, not fewer, of these crimes are being committed, but people aren't reporting them. In most cases they have to do it online, and they end up not doing it. They don't believe anything will happen, so don't see the point. And they're right."[283]

Some believe that the surge in automobile break-ins in San Francisco can be blamed on Prop. 47. Certainly, the timing is right. Meanwhile, one San Francisco resident complained that "every bicycle in our building has been stolen" while criminal activity near the home of an elderly gentleman who has lived in San Francisco all his life has become so unbearable that he feels as if he's imprisoned in his own home.[284]

"I've caught so many people stealing packages. They don't care. They know nothing will happen to them. It's crazy. It's horrible. I feel like these people need to go to jail," Karen Burns, president of a San Francisco condominium association, said in January 2018.[285]

TABLE 5: CALIFORNIA RATES FOR PROPERTY CRIME (INCIDENTS PER 100,000 POPULATION)

The same pattern of falling property crime has also been seen in the rate, particularly burglary, which has dropped sharply since 2012

	TOTAL PROPERTY CRIMES	BURGLARY	LARCENY-THEFT	MOTOR-VEHICLE THEFT
2010	2,630.1	612.8	1,608.7	408.6
2011	2,593.7	612.9	1,589.5	391.3
2012	2,772.6	649.3	1,677.8	445.5
2013	2,665.5	607	1,626	432.5
2014	2,459	526.1	1,538.6	394.3
2015	2,620.4	504.7	1,678.6	437.1
2016	2,554.5	478.1	1,617.5	448.9
2017	2,491	445.9	1,620.2	424.9

Source: Crime in California 2017, California Department Of Justice, California Justice Information Services Division, Bureau Of Criminal Information And Analysis, Criminal Justice Statistics Center, Table 1, Page 6

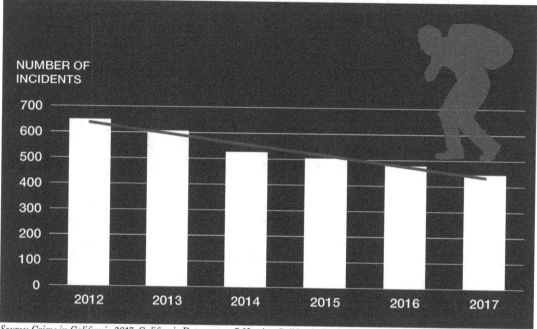

CALIFORNIA BURGLARY RATES HAVE DROPPED SHARPLY

NUMBER OF
INCIDENTS

Source: Crime in California 2017, California Department Of Justice, California Justice Information Services Division, Bureau Of Criminal Information And Analysis, Criminal Justice Statistics Center, Table 1, Page 6

A University of California, Irvine, study says that these observations are wrong, that any blame placed on Prop. 47 is misplaced. Charis Kubrin, a professor of criminology, law and society, and Bradley Bartos, a doctoral student in criminology, law and society, compared the state's 2015 crime rates to those of a manufactured control group called "synthetic California." This "synthetic control group" was used "to approximate California crime rates had Proposition 47 not been enacted." "Our findings suggest Proposition 47 is not responsible for increases in homicide, rape, aggravated assault or robbery," the researchers said. "While our findings appear to show that larceny and motor vehicle thefts increased following Proposition 47's enactment, these findings don't hold up to additional testing."[286]

The study does not include the 2016 data, however, which show a 4.9 percent increase in the violent crime rate over 2015 and a 12.5 percent increase over 2011. Nor does it include the 2017 data, which also show increases in the rate of violent crime from 2016 to 2017 (2.2 percent) and 2012 to 2017 (11.2 percent). A more recent study by the Public Policy Institute of California, published in January 2018, says that "The effects of post-realignment reforms, including Proposition 47, remain unknown."[287]

Proposition 57

Police say that in April 2013, Daniel William Marsh, who was 15 years old, killed an elderly Davis couple in their bed. Musician Oliver Northup, 87, and his wife, 76-year-old church official Claudia Maupin, were stabbed to death in a "case that stunned Davis and Yolo County for its savagery," the *Sacramento Bee* reported. The victims were "slashed and mutilated" as they slept.[288]

"That night I couldn't take it anymore. I had to do it. I was looking around to see which house I should go into," Marsh told police. "It felt amazing." Marsh, who had prowled his neighborhood for targets, also told them that "It felt great. It was pure happiness. It was the most enjoyable feeling I've ever felt."[289]

"Never have I seen such a heinous and reprehensible act, and never have I seen a defendant with such an evil soul," Michael Cabral, a former assistant chief deputy district attorney for Yolo County who was the lead prosecutor in the case.[290]

Marsh was tried as an adult and convicted and sentenced to 52 years to life. He has been serving out the sentence in the R.J. Donovan Correctional Facility in San Diego. But a February 2018 appellate court set a hearing for later in the year that would decide if Marsh should be retried in juvenile court, based on a February 2018 California Supreme Court decision that ruled a new state law could be applied retroactively. If so, Marsh "could only be detained until he reaches the age of 25," according to Yolo County District Attorney Jeff Reisig.[291]

"In October 2018, Yolo Superior Court Judge Samuel McAdam ruled that Marsh could not be tried as a juvenile."[292]

> Proposition 57, known as the "The Public Safety and Rehabilitation Act of 2016," was a further attempt to cut the state prison population, coming two years after Proposition 47.

Then there's the case of Alfredo "Freddy" Casillas, who was sentenced in 1988 to 16 years to life for a 1985 murder in Burbank. Michele Hanisee, president of the Association of Deputy District Attorneys for Los Angeles County, told the story in *CityWatch*:

> In September of 1992, while still serving his murder sentence, Casillas slashed another inmate three times with a prison-made weapon. Then, in May of 1994, Casillas attacked another inmate with a spear/arrow

type weapon, hitting the other inmate in the head. Casillas was sentenced to eight years for these assaults, to run consecutive to his murder sentence. The Parole Board granted Casillas parole on his murder in January of 2015, but Casillas was not released as he still had to serve the consecutive eight years for the assaults. In January of 2018, although Casillas had only served three years of this eight-year term, the Parole Board released Casillas early, after determining that he "did not pose an unreasonable risk of violence to the community if released."[293]

Nicholas Joseph Davanzo, was sent to prison in 2014, convicted of assault with force likely to produce great bodily injury for attacking his girlfriend. The sentence was eight years. There were also two felony convictions on his record in the previous three years. Davanzo's parole review indicated that his "current commitment offense aggravate the inmate's current risk of violence." His victim asked that he not be granted early release. Yet his early release for parole was approved in January 2018.[294, 295]

These are the types of outcomes that Proposition 57 opponents feared.

Though approved by a wide margin, Prop. 57, tagged by some as a get-of-jail-early card, had many vocal opponents.

Prop. 57, known as the "The Public Safety and Rehabilitation Act of 2016," was a further attempt to cut the state prison population, coming two years after Prop. 47. Passed by a roughly 64-36 margin, and effective upon its Nov. 9, 2016, approval, this ballot measure was intended to: protect and enhance public safety; save money by cutting wasteful prison spending; stop federal courts from indiscriminately releasing prisoners; end the "revolving door" of crime by focusing on rehabilitation, particularly for juvenile offenders; and require judges rather than prosecutors to determine when juveniles should be tried as adults.[296]

To achieve these goals, it allows any inmate convicted of a non-violent felony offense and sentenced to state prison to seek parole consideration after the full term of the inmate's primary offense is completed. It also gives the Department of Corrections and Rehabilitation the authority to award credits earned for good behavior as well as rehabilitative or educational achievements, such as academic programs, substance-abuse treatment programs, social life-skills courses, and career technical education classes.[297] The credits became a source of concern for some who believed that the program focuses more on participation in the activities rather than completion or meeting meaningful milestones and benchmarks.

Supporters promised that Prop. 57 would at the same time reduce the state's prison population while also increasing public safety.

"Eighty percent of what Prop. 57 does is being done right now under the force of a court order. It is backed up by the United States Supreme Court and which we cannot change unless they say our remedy, in this case Proposition 57, is durable and serves the end of justice," Then-Gov. Jerry Brown said two months before the vote.[298]

"I think, if anything, this is the greatest step we could take for public safety in California," he added.[299]

In an editorial urging voters to approve the measure, the *Los Angeles Times* called it a "much-needed check on prosecutorial power."

"Inmates will have new incentives to change their behavior, both in prison and after release. For many inmates, prisons will cease to be merely warehouses and may at last become instruments of rehabilitation."[300]

CALmatters characterized the support in this way: Advocates see it as "a long-term solution that stops wasting costly prison space on non-violent offenders who can be rehabilitated, while keeping dangerous criminals behind bars. It gives judges — instead of prosecutors — the power to decide whether a minor should be tried as an adult, which will improve juvenile justice by reducing racial bias and the number of minors sent through adult courts."[301]

Though approved by a wide margin, Prop. 57, tagged by some as a get-of-jail-early card, had many vocal opponents. The *San Diego Union-Tribune* editorial board, which has criticized the state's "tough-on-crime policies from the 1990s" because they "have led tens of thousands of people with salvageable lives to be warehoused in prison long after they posed a likely public threat," calls Prop. 57 "a deeply flawed measure."

The problem, said the *Union-Tribune*, was that under the measure "such brutal crimes as rape of an unconscious person or violent child abuse were classified as 'nonviolent.' That's because they were not included among the crimes specified as violent felonies in section 667.5 of the California Penal Code."[302]

The credits became a source of concern for some who believed that the program focuses more on participation in the activities rather than completion or meeting meaningful milestones and benchmarks.

Columnist Debra J. Saunders called it "the sort of dishonest measure that becomes commonplace under unaccountable one-party rule" before it was approved at the polls. According to Saunders, "Prop. 57 peels back" the public protections from multiple offenders, such as 1994's "three strikes" law, which she believes are in part responsible for California's crime rates having been "low over the past decade."[303]

Saunders further noted that former GOP Gov. Pete Wilson "fears Prop. 57 will take California back to the 1970s, when crime was so scary that San Francisco's best-known movie cop was Clint Eastwood's Dirty Harry. After a shootout, the detective would ask bad guys if they wanted to bet whether a bullet was left in his .44 Magnum: 'Do you feel lucky?' . . . Do you feel lucky, voter?"[304]

The Association of Deputy District Attorneys for Los Angeles County published a fact sheet for Prop. 57 which said the measure would allow:

- Offenders who have committed multiple crimes against multiple victims to be eligible for release at the same time as offenders who have committed single crimes against single victims.

- Repeat offenders to be eligible for release after the same period of incarceration as first-time offenders.

- Offenders whose sentences were enhanced due to especially egregious conduct to be eligible for release at the same time as those who did not engage in the egregious conduct.

- The California Department of Corrections and Rehabilitation to have unlimited authority to award credits to all inmates, in excess of the current 15 percent, 20 percent and 50 percent conduct credit limitations.

- Juvenile offenders who commit violent crimes such as murder, rape, and carjacking to avoid being filed on as adults.[305]

The fact sheet also contends that Prop. 57 not only fails to define which crimes qualify as "non-violent" felonies, there is no "existing code section (to) define or list what crimes qualify as 'non-violent.'" The sole existing definition of what constitutes a violent felony can be found with (Penal Code Section) 667.5.[306] That leaves the following crimes to be open to consideration as "non-violent felonies":

- Battery that includes serious bodily injury
- Solicitation to commit murder
- Domestic violence

- Inflicting corporal injury on a child

- First-degree burglary

- Rape/sodomy/oral copulation of unconscious person or by use of date-rape drugs

- Human trafficking involving a minor

- Hate crimes

- Arson of forest land that causes physical injury

- Assault on a peace officer with a deadly weapon

- Active participation in a street gang

- Exploding destructive device with intent to cause injury[307]

The California District Attorneys Association issued similar warnings. In a report written for the governor's review, the organization said the change in eligibility for parole "disregards enhancements such as use of a deadly weapon, commission of a crime to benefit a criminal street gang, or prior prison terms; disregards consecutive sentences for the commission of multiple offenses; and provides prison officials with broad authority to award increased conduct credits, including to murderers and rapists."[308]

"The Act significantly undermines more than four decades of criminal justice policies approved by the Legislature and California voters that were designed to enhance public safety and protect the rights of crime victims."[309]

The California District Attorneys Association also argued that the law's title, purpose, and intent are misleading; the process that produced it lacked input and transparency; and the act itself conflicts with other initiatives and statutes. It also creates multiple uncertainties concerning parole procedure and practice and, in the end, "will jeopardize rather than protect public safety."[310]

> During the Prop. 57 campaign, critics pointed out that its language was so broad that convicted sex offenders would be among those eligible for early release.

The intent of the initiative appears to be to accelerate the release of state prison inmates serving terms for non-violent offenses. But it does so with a sledge hammer rather than a scalpel, amending the Constitution to drastically reduce sentences by requiring parole consideration for those serving consecutive sentences for multiple crimes, repeat offenders, and those whose crimes are aggravated by factors resulting in enhancements. Moreover, the initiative is drafted in a manner that may well make it applicable to serious felonies, violent felonies and possibly even murders. The credits provisions violate the intent of the Legislature and the voters in requiring inmates to actually serve the sentences they receive.[311]

Prop. 57 has not been in effect long enough for a comprehensive study of its effects to be done. But that will eventually change. As of Jan. 1, 2018, the state Board of Parole Hearings had "reviewed the cases of thousands of eligible inmates and granted parole for more than 600," the *San Diego Union-Tribune* reported in early 2018. "Among them were people convicted of burglary, drug crimes, vehicle theft, grand theft, elder abuse, vandalism and other crimes."[312]

David Greenberg, a chief deputy in the San Diego district attorney's office, says that, "we'll see what the folks do who got out early, see how well they behave. I'm concerned that some folks who get early release due to Prop. 57 will victimize people again."[313]

Many others could be released under Prop. 57, as well. Janice Bellucci, a Sacramento attorney who is president of California Reform Sex Offender Laws, now known as the Alliance for Constitutional Sex Offense Laws, sued the state on behalf of sex offenders. The lawsuit "argued that the rules conflict with the ballot measure's language and voters' intent in approving Proposition 57," the Associated Press reported in February 2018. "Bellucci argued the measure requires earlier parole consideration for any sex crime not on the state's narrow list of 23 violent felonies, which includes murder, kidnapping and forcible rape."[314]

During the Prop. 57 campaign, critics pointed out that its language was so broad that convicted sex offenders would be among those eligible for early release. Former Gov. Brown, however, promised that sex offenders would be excluded from consideration for early release. He even signed a statement, which "said Proposition 57 would not and will not 'change the federal court order that excludes sex offenders, as defined in Penal Code 290, from parole.' "[315] The state argued that it had wide latitude to exclude non-violent sex offenses even if they weren't excluded by the language of the law. Those crimes include "raping a drugged or unconscious victim, intimately touching someone who is unlawfully restrained, incest, pimping a minor, indecent exposure and possessing child pornography," the AP reported.

Early in 2018, Sacramento County Superior Court Judge Allen Sumner issued a preliminary order directing the state to revise the rules for administering Proposition 57. "If the voters had intended to exclude all registered sex offenders from early parole consideration under Proposition 57, they presumably would have said so," Sumner said.[316]

Sumner's ruling could mean "earlier parole for more than half of the 20,000 sex offenders now serving time."[317]

REFORM RECOMMENDATIONS FOR PROPOSITIONS 47 AND 57:

The language of the proposed Reducing Crime and Keeping California Safe Act, submitted for a ballot initiative for November 2020, says its purpose is to "fix three related problems created by recent laws that have threatened the public safety of Californians and their children from violent criminals . . . A. Reform the parole system so violent felons are not released early from prison . . . B. Reform theft laws to restore accountability for serial thieves and organized theft rings; . . . C. Expand DNA collection from persons convicted of drug, theft and domestic violence related crimes to help solve violent crimes and exonerate the innocent."[318]

Some parts of the Reducing Crime and Keeping California Safe Act have merit. Expanding the catalog of violent crimes whose violators should not be considered for early release is a rational response to the flaws that have plagued some of the state's criminal justice reorganizations. It is in the best interest of public safety, and it should be non-controversial, that those who have:

> engaged in the human trafficking of children, abducted a minor for prostitution, raped an intoxicated or unconscious victim, committed a drive-by shooting, solicited for murder, caused great physical injury during a felony assault, attacked another with a caustic chemical, taken a hostage to avoid arrest, caused death or serious injury when resisting a law enforcement officer, exploded a bomb to injure others, committed a felony with a deadly weapon, used felonious force to threaten a victim or witness, and committed felony elder abuse[319]

should not be released early from their prison terms as they are eligible under current law. Lawmakers are obligated to make the changes necessary to prevent these offenders from hitting the streets before they have served the appropriate terms of their sentences.

Because it changed several felonies to misdemeanors, Prop. 47 has led to a decline in the DNA samples that could be collected from offenders by law enforcement authorities. Lawmakers from both parties have supported reinstating the practice. It is a provision of the Reducing Crime and Keeping California Safe Act. But it is not so clear that the positives would outweigh the negatives. For instance, DNA collection is more intrusive than fingerprinting. Samples are typically obtained by swabbing the inside of the cheek. Should low-level non-violent offenders guilty of misdemeanors be subject to that practice just as a serious offender would?

Under the Reducing Crime and Keeping California Safe Act, misdemeanants guilty of low-level ($950 or less) shoplifting, forgery, writing bad checks, receiving stolen property, disorderly conduct,[320] and the unauthorized use of a vehicle,[321] as well as several other misdemeanors, would be subject to DNA collection. The offenses for which DNA is collected should be limited to more serious crimes where there is more at stake.

Other policymaking priorities include:

Establishing serial thefts as felonies. Prop. 47 virtually invited shoplifters and thieves to engage in a "merry-go-round of plunder." "Since 2014, we've seen a significant increase in both incidents and in the value of cases as it became known that no matter how many times you're caught – so long as you stay under $950 – you'll just get a citation to show up in court," says Aaron Moreno, the California Grocers Association senior director for government relations.[322] Fresno Police Chief Jerry Dyer says Prop. 47 has emboldened the careers of small-time criminals because there are "no consequences" for their actions.

"There's an individual we have arrested 83 times since Prop. 47 has passed, all on petty thefts, 83 times," he said in July 2018.[323]

Closing Proposition 57's sex offender loophole. The list of crimes considered violent under Prop. 57 needs to be expanded. It "left way too much wiggle room," said Mark Zahner, chief executive of the California District Attorneys Association. "There's a great danger of truly violent people being released early and people who commit, in this case, sex offenses that involve violence being released early."[324]

Closing Proposition 57's assault with a deadly weapon and drive-by shootings loophole. Clarity is needed on these and several other offenses that have been deemed "non-violent" under the measure.

Private Prisons

About 4,000 inmates are serving California sentences in private prisons. It's roughly a 50-50 split between in-state private facilities, and private prisons in Arizona.[325] Privately run facilities are a safety valve for the state's overcrowded prison conditions that are being underutilized, and they are also central in halting the revolving door that puts many offenders back in prison after release.

"Through improvements to inmate education and re-entry programs, private prisons are helping develop solutions aimed at reducing recidivism rates and thus the prison population," Reason Foundation policy analyst Austill Stuart wrote in 2017.[326]

The success can be seen in Orange County, where there are two privately operated "day reporting centers" which are "tasked with managing former inmates' experiences as they transition back to living in the community. Think of these centers as one-stop shops offering access to the sorts of social services and other offerings needed to help people get back on their feet."[327]

Stuart says, "the California Department of Corrections and Rehabilitation's most recent Outcome Evaluation Report found Orange County had the second lowest recidivism rate in the state, ahead of every county except Los Angeles County."[328]

Privately run prisons are also more financially responsible than state-run facilities. The state spends $75,560 a year to house prisoners in its own facilities, the highest per-inmate cost in the country,[329] while the cost of housing a California inmate in a private prison is roughly half that.[330]

The case against private prisons is simply not as clear as their opponents claim it is.

Despite the advantages that private prisons have over government-run facilities, lawmakers want to sever the state's ties to out-of-state private prisons. In 2017, the Legislature passed Assembly Bill 1320, which would:

> Prohibit the department from entering into a contract with an out-of-state, private, for-profit prison on or after January 1, 2018, and would prohibit the department from renewing a contract with an out-of-state, private, for-profit prison on or after January 1, 2020. The bill would also prohibit, after January 1, 2021, any state prison inmate or other person under the jurisdiction of the department from being housed in any out-of-state, private, for-profit prison facility.[331]

Former Gov. Brown vetoed the bill, not because he believes private prisons are useful and should not be dismissed as an option, but because that in order "to maintain the prison population at or below 137.5 percent of design capacity, as required by the federal courts, the Department of Corrections and Rehabilitation need to maintain maximum flexibility in the short term."[332]

Legislation introduced for the 2019 session, Assembly Bill 32, is intended to halt the state from entering into new contracts or renewing existing contracts with private prisons beginning in January 2020. It would further prohibit any California inmate from being incarcerated at a private facility after January 1, 2028.[333]

REFORM RECOMMENDATIONS:
State should embrace private incarceration facilities

Incarcerating inmates in prisons run by the state of California carries a staggering cost. Inmates can be housed at much less cost to the taxpayers in private facilities. Given this, and the research finding that private prisons "don't clearly provide worse quality"[334] than government-run prisons, there's no reason to exclude them from the corrections system.

In the instances when there are clear problems in private facilities, policymakers should pursue what law professor Sasha Volokh calls the "mend it, don't end it" approach. He believes "performance-based contracting has the potential to open up new vistas of quality improvements."[335]

An additional reason for the state to continue, and even increase, the use of private prisons is their availability to quickly deal with overcrowding in other facilities. They are sensible safety valves.

It also needs to be noted that while prison systems in the United States in general and in California specifically are routinely criticized for what some consider the brutal treatment of inmates, many other nations, including several whose corrections systems have reputations for exercising more restraint than American justice, have been increasing their use of private prisons.

The case against private prisons is simply not as clear as their opponents claim it is. Legislators need to keep their minds open and rethink their position on private prisons based on the evidence at hand before they again bring up legislation to cut ties with out-of-state facilities.

Restorative Justice

Restorative justice as a system "seeks to repair the harm done to all parties affected by crime – the victim, the community, and the offender; to hold offenders accountable; and to improve community safety, while increasing the ability of the youth who comes into contact with the juvenile justice system to contribute to his or her family and society," according to a handbook published by the state's Administrative Office of the Courts.[336]

> A crime is seen as an act against an individual victim or victims and the community. Restorative justice emphasizes the impact of crime or wrongdoing on relationships. Restorative justice is focused on addressing the needs of the most affected parties rather than simply ensuring that offenders get what they deserve.[337]

Yolo County District Attorney Jeff Reisig released in August 2017 a report that covered the first four years of the "victim-centric," "voluntary and confidential" Yolo County Neighborhood Court, in which:

> Volunteer panelists take part in a conference with their fellow community members and the participant to hold them accountable by identifying the harms caused by their conduct. Together they come up with a collaborative solution designed to address those harms in a way that is restorative rather than punitive.[338]

The report's findings included an independent evaluation that determined the recidivism rate for participants was 4 percent.

"As NHC has grown, from an innovative idea, to a rapidly expanding alternative, to an increasingly mature program, the program has continued to seek and do justice – by providing an alternative option for eligible individuals. . . . NHC strives to remain victim-centric, and provide direct victims with the specialized attention necessary to understand their rights, options, and resources within and outside of the program, as well as providing the opportunity for all parties to voice their thoughts and concerns."[339]

Economists Bryan Caplan and Edward P. Stringham note that "over the last three decades, however, researchers from across the political spectrum have questioned the idea that all law comes from the state."[340] Policymakers need to remember that in their efforts to reduce crime.

> Sometimes criminal activity can be appropriately resolved by the private sector - not with vigilantism, but through a cooperative system in which both victims and offenders reach an agreement that works for both parties.

REFORM RECOMMENDATIONS:
State should embrace private sector restorative justice programs

Sometimes criminal activity can be appropriately resolved by the private sector - not with vigilantism, but through a cooperative system in which both victims and offenders reach an agreement that works for both parties.

California retailers lose as much as $4 billion each year to shoplifting, about $11 million a day. The public loses, too, as shoplifting depletes law enforcement and judicial resources, and raises prices for consumers, and retailers pass on the costs of increased security and lost inventory. One such private-sector program offers offenders a shot at redemption that doesn't exist in the criminal court system, and also satisfies victims, is operated by the Corrective Education Company.[341]

Under this program, shoplifters who are caught by store security staff are offered two choices: they can sign a confession and voluntarily enter a program in which they are taught a life-skills course, or they are free to take their chances in the criminal justice system. Shoplifters who choose corrective education pay a $400 fee for the cost of the class, or $500 if they must pay over time. Those who cannot afford the fee can take advantage of scholarships. In some instances, offenders pay nothing.[342]

The program has a record of success. The data show that 90 percent of those who are offered the course choose to enter it. The recidivism rate among those is less than 2 percent while outside the program the rate is as high as 80 percent.[343]

Walmart, the world's largest retailer, which has 306 stores in California,[344] has used restorative justice program and apparently found it to be effective.

"The alternative to prosecution is an opportunity to be rehabbed through essentially an online course . . . that's about eight hours in duration," Mike Lamb, then vice president of Walmart's Asset Protection and Safety, said in 2017. "We've seen a dramatic reduction in recidivism or repeat offense scenarios for those individuals who have successfully completed the program."[345]

Skidmore College sociology professor David Karpnotes that if Walmart "can reduce shoplifting by helping people understand the costs to the company as well as to themselves, that's a good thing."[346] "I think," he said, "Walmart recognizes that sending them to jail isn't particularly productive."[347]

The program, which an estimated 13,000 Californians have completed, is no longer an option in the state, however. San Francisco Superior Court Judge Harold Kahn killed the program in 2017, calling it a "textbook extortion under California law" and "false imprisonment" when ruling in a lawsuit brought by San Francisco City Attorney Dennis Herrera against the Corrective Education Company.[348] The ruling both restricts choice – 90 percent of offenders choose private restorative-justice programs over criminal courts – and hurts efforts to reduce crime – the recidivism rate for those who enter the programs is 2 percent compared to 80 percent for those who don't.[349]

Restorative justice can also play a role in keeping juveniles on the right road. Lisa Weinreb, chief of the San Diego district attorney's juvenile branch, believes in the National Conflict Resolution Center. "The NCRC has done a fantastic job," she says. "We've attended some of the circles and are impressed with the whole process in terms in how it is helping the youth."[350]

A program administered by the NCRC was established in San Diego by the Restorative Community Conferencing Pilot Program in 2014. The *California Health Report* says a restorative community conference under the program "involves the youth responsible for the crime, the person(s) harmed by the crime, advocates for both the responsible youth and the victim(s), members of the community, and at least one trained restorative justice facilitator."[351]

Through November 2017, the program had accepted 122 juveniles, 68 of whom had by then completed the process. The one-year recidivism rate for those who finished "is about half that of those who did not participate in the program," says the *California Health Report.*[352]

The success warrants both an experimental expansion of the current program as well consideration by other jurisdictions to creating their own pilot programs.

Restorative justice legislation passed and signed in 2016, Assembly Bill 2590 authored by Assemblywoman Shirley Weber, D-San Diego, deserves, as well, ongoing evaluation from policymakers to determine if it will be effective. While it's too new to decide if it will be a valuable tool, it might have a fatal flaw: those convicted of sex offenses are eligible for alternative adjudication under AB 2590,[353] which "provides an opportunity for the offender to accept responsibility, acknowledge the harm, make agreements to repair the damages as much as possible and clarify intentions."[354]

Bail Reform

Veteran California columnist Dan Walters wrote in late 2017 that "the next big criminal justice issue" will be bail reform.

"A coalition of penal reform organizations is backing legislation by Sen. Bob Hertzberg, a Van Nuys Democrat, aimed at reducing the number of those facing criminal charges who are locked up because they can't post bail," says Walters.[355]

Hertzberg claims that "California's current money bail system comes at great cost not only to the detained individual and his or her family but also to California communities. When wealth and charges alone determine whether or not someone will be released pending trial, community safety suffers."[356]

In the 2017-18 session, Hertzberg introduced Senate Bill 10, which eliminates cash bail schedules and also transfer to county pretrial-service agencies, and away from judges, the authority to determine how much risk a suspect poses to the community. Hertzberg's bill eventually passed, was signed by Former Gov. Brown in August 2018, and was to take effect in October 2019. However, a referendum to overturn the law will appear on the 2020 election ballot. Opponents say the legislation is a threat to public safety, as it releases offenders who pose a high risk to the community back into the streets.

The Judicial Council of California, which makes the rules for the state's court system, has expressed procedural concerns with the law, including its "impact on judicial discretion and independence; the creation of unrealistic or unspecified timelines; the imposition of unrealistic responsibilities and expectations on the pretrial services agencies that courts would rely on for information in making decisions, and the creation of an overly burdensome and complicated system."[357]

While the bill was making its way through the legislative system, Lipstick Bail Bonds from Southern California said that the proposed reform "has set the stage to make California the fugitive capital of the world." Duane Chapman, known to the television audience as Dog the Bounty Hunter, told lawmakers during a 2017 hearing the legislation could "let lawbreakers go home and say they're poor."[358]

The history of the accused being released on bail shows that it was created to protect the poor, not exploit them. Bail was established "to balance the playing field among the rich, middle, and poor classes when individuals were accused of a crime." Before bail was employed by the courts, "only those who had enough money and property to post a security were lucky enough to secure temporary release pending their trials."[359]

REFORM RECOMMENDATIONS:
Keep an eye on the East Coast

Before lawmakers passed the bill, they should have watched how events were playing out in New Jersey, which virtually eliminated cash bail on Jan. 1, 2017. If they had waited, New Jersey would have eventually recorded enough data to show if released arrestees were failing to appear in greater numbers than before – which is what critics are expecting – and if violent crime increased – which happened in New Mexico after bail reform there.[360] That lawmakers would choose this course at a time when crime is increasing might prove to be unwise. But it might not get that far. Their decision might be overridden by Californians, who will be able to draw on New Jersey's experience when they vote on the 2020 referendum to overturn the law.

Conclusion

There's no reason that increased public safety and reasonable criminal justice can't live side by side in California. But lawmakers cannot let the pendulum swing too far one way or the other. There must be a balance between the state's obligation to victims, as well as its duty to reduce the number of future victims, and the rights of the accused and convicted. California has long been known as a state that innovates. Policymakers should be searching for ground-breaking ideas while keeping in place established practices that have proved to be effective. And they must do it as cost-effectively as possible.

Appendix:
Selected California and National Crime Data and Trends

PERCENT RATE INCREASES AND DECREASES FOR VIOLENT CRIMES, CRIMES PER 100,000 POPULATION

	ALL VIOLENT CRIMES	HOMICIDE	ROBBERY	AGGRAVATED ASSAULT
2012 to 2017	6.1	-8	-4.3	6.6

Sources: Crime in California 2017, California Department of Justice, California Justice Information Services Division, Bureau of Criminal Information and Analysis, Criminal Justice Statistics Center, Table 2; Crime in California 2016, California Department of Justice, California Justice Information Services Division, Bureau of Criminal Information and Analysis, Criminal Justice Statistics Center, Table 2

PERCENT RATE INCREASES AND DECREASES FOR PROPERTY CRIMES, CRIMES PER 100,000 POPULATION

	ALL PROPERTY CRIMES	BURGLARY	MOTOR VEHICLE THEFT	LARCENY-THEFT
2012 to 2017	-10.2	-31.3	-4.6	-3.4

Sources: Crime in California 2017, California Department of Justice, California Justice Information Services Division, Bureaus of Criminal Information and Analysis, Criminal Justice Statistics Center, Table 2; Crime in California 2016, California Department of Justice, California Justice Information Services Division, Bureaus of Criminal Information and Analysis, Criminal Justice Statistics Center, Table 2

NATIONAL RATES FOR VIOLENT CRIME
(INCIDENTS PER 100,000 POPULATION)
After falling earlier in the decade, the violent crime rate has increased in two of the last three years

	TOTAL VIOLENT CRIME	MURDER/ NONNEGLIGENT MANSLAUGHTER	ROBBERY	AGGRAVATED ASSAULT
2010	404.5	4.8	119.3	252.8
2011	387.1	4.7	113.9	241.5
2012	387.8	4.7	113.1	242.8
2013	369.1	4.5	109	229.6
2014	361.6	4.4	101.3	229.2
2015	373.7	4.9	102.2	238.1
2016	386.6	5.4	102.9	248.3
2017	382.9	5.3	98	248.9

Source: Crime in the United States 2017, U.S. Department of Justice, Federal Bureau of Investigation, Criminal Justice Information Services Division, Table 1

NATIONWIDE VIOLENT CRIME ON RISE AFTER YEARS OF DECLINE

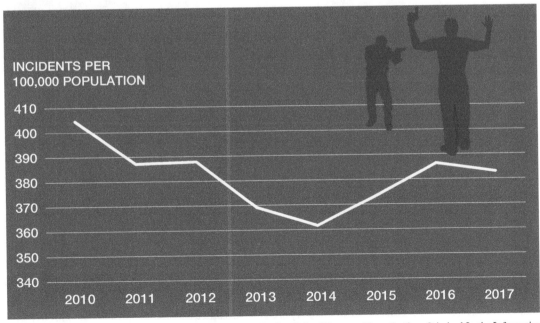

Source: Crime in the United States 2017, U.S. Department of Justice, Federal Bureau of Investigation, Criminal Justice Information Services Division, Table 1

NATIONAL RATES FOR PROPERTY CRIME
(INCIDENTS PER 100,000 POPULATION)

National rates for most property crimes continue to fall, but motor-vehicle theft has risen for three straight years

	TOTAL PROPERTY CRIMES	BURGLARY	LARCENY-THEFT	MOTOR-VEHICLE THEFT
2010	2,945.9	701	2,005.8	239.1
2011	2,905.4	701.3	1,974.1	230
2012	2,868	672.2	1,965.4	230.4
2013	2,733.6	610.5	1,901.9	221.3
2014	2,574.1	537.2	1,821.5	215.4
2015	2,500.5	494.7	1,783.6	222.2
2016	2,451.6	468.9	1,745.4	237.3
2017	2,362.2	430.4	1,694.4	237.4

MOTOR VEHICLE THEFT ON RISE RATIONALLY, DESPITE OVERALL FALL IN PROPERTY CRIME RATES

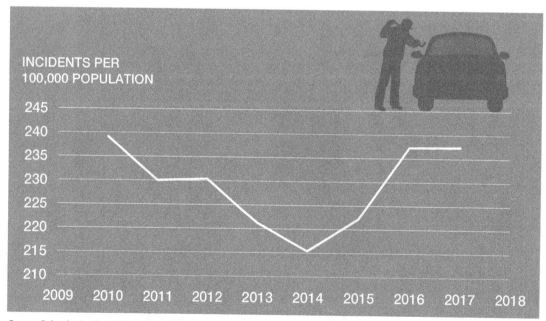

Source: Crime in the United States 2017, U.S. Department of Justice, Federal Bureau of Investigation, Criminal Justice Information Services Division, Table 1

CALIFORNIA VIOLENT CRIME
Overall violent crime in California has increased over the last three years, led by aggravated assault, which grew by nearly 14 percent from 2014 to 2016, and increased again in 2017

	TOTAL VIOLENT CRIME	HOMICIDE	ROBBERY	AGGRAVATED ASSAULT
2010	163,957	1,809	58,100	95,723
2011	155,313	1,794	54,358	91,483
2012	160,629	1,878	56,491	94,432
2013	151,634	1,745	53,621	88,809
2014	151,425	1,697	48,650	91,681
2015	166,588	1,861	52,785	99,149
2016	174,701	1,930	54,769	104,307
2017	178,553	1,829	56,609	105,391

Source: Open Justice, California Department of Justice, Data Exploration, Crime Statistics, Crimes and Clearances

VIOLENT CRIME ON RISE IN CALIFORNIA, LED BY INCREASES IN AGGRAVATED ASSAULT

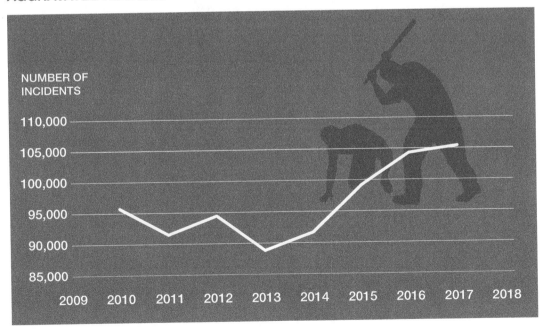

Source: Open Justice, California Department of Justice, Data Exploration, Crime Statistics, Crimes and Clearances

CALIFORNIA RATES FOR VIOLENT CRIME
(INCIDENTS PER 100,000 POPULATION)
California's violent crime rate has increased in recent years, as well

	TOTAL VIOLENT CRIME	HOMICIDE	ROBBERY	AGGRAVATED ASSAULT
2010	439.3	4.8	155.7	256.5
2011	413.3	4.8	144.7	243.4
2012	424.7	5	149.3	249.6
2013	396.9	4.6	140.4	232.5
2014	393.3	4.4	126.4	238.1
2015	426.4	4.8	135.1	253.8
2016	443.9	4.9	139.2	265
2017	450.7	4.6	142.9	266.1

Source: Crime in California 2017, California Department Of Justice, California Justice Information Services Division, Bureau Of Criminal Information And Analysis, Criminal Justice Statistics Center, Table 1, Page 6

VIOLENT CRIME ON RISE IN CALIFORNIA

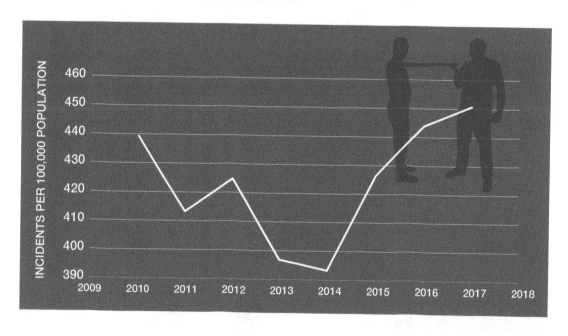

CALIFORNIA PROPERTY CRIME
Meanwhile, as violent crime across the state increases, the major property crimes are falling

	TOTAL PROPERTY CRIMES	BURGLARY	LARCENY-THEFT	MOTOR- VEHICLE THEFT
2010	981,523	228,672	600,357	152,494
2011	974,666	230,334	597,302	147,030
2012	1,948,764	245,601	634,647	168,516
2013	1,108,946	231,909	621,207	165,217
2014	946,582	202,556	592,336	151,790
2015	1,023,828	197,189	655,851	170,788
2016	1,001,380	188,162	636,542	176,676
2017	986,769	176,638	641,804	168,327

Source: Open Justice, California Department of Justice, Data Exploration, Crime Statistics, Crimes and Clearances

CALIFORNIA MOTOR-VEHICLE THEFT DECLINES AFTER RISING THREE STRAIGHT YEARS

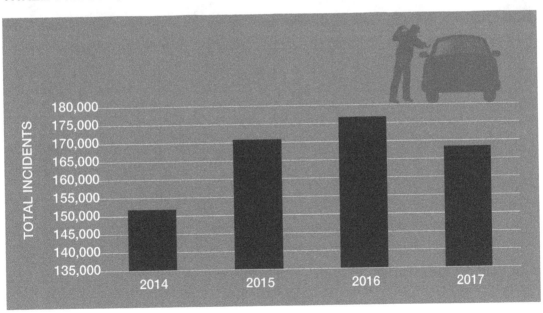

SHARP INCREASE IN RAPE CASES STATEWIDE FOLLOWING YEARS OF STEADY DECLINE

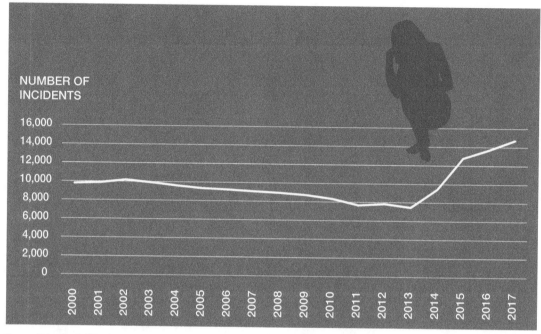

Source: Crime in California 2017, California Department Of Justice, California Justice Information Services Division, Bureau Of Criminal Information And Analysis, Criminal Justice Statistics Center, Table 1, Pages 5-6

RAPE IN CALIFORNIA SINCE 2000

Total incidents of rape as well as the rate fell steadily throughout the 2000s and into the 2010s until there was a sharp increase in both beginning in 2014 that continued into 2017

	TOTAL	INCIDENTS PER 100,000 POPULATION
2017	14,724	37.2
2016	13,695	34.8
2015	12,793	32.7
2014	9,397	24.4
2013	7,459	19.5
2012	7,828	20.7
2011	7,678	20.4
2010	8,325	22.3
2009	8,698	23.5
2008	8,906	24.2
2007	9,047	24.8
2006	9,213	25.4
2005	9,345	26
2004	9,598	26.8
2003	9,918	28
2002	10,176	29.1
2001	9,882	28.6
2000	9,785	28.8

Source: Crime in California 2017, California Department Of Justice, California Justice Information Services Division, Bureau Of Criminal Information And Analysis, Criminal Justice Statistics Center, Table 1, Pages 5-6

Endnotes

1   Max Ehrenfreund, "California is about to learn that 'tough on crime' is tough to undo," *Washington Post*, November 6, 2014, https://www.washingtonpost.com/news/wonk/wp/2014/11/06/wonkbook-california-is-about-to-learn-that-tough-on-crime-is-tough-to-undo/.

2   Laura Gottesdiener, "California Prison Legislation Is Among The Most Punitive In The Nation," *Huffington Post*, July 27, 2011, https://www.huffingtonpost.com/2011/05/27/california-prison-legislation_n_868326.html.

3   Description of *Three Strikes and the Politics of Crime in America's Golden State*, accessed October 29, 2018, https://www.ucpress.edu/book.php?isbn=9780520246683.

4   Evelyn Nieves, "California's Governor Plays Tough on Crime," *New York Times*, May 23, 2000, https://www.nytimes.com/2000/05/23/us/california-s-governor-plays-tough-on-crime.html.

5   "Crime in the United States 2012," U.S. Department of Justice, Federal Bureau of Investigation, Criminal Justice Information Services Division, Table 1, accessed October 29, 2018, https://ucr.fbi.gov/crime-in-the-u.s/2012/crime-in-the-u.s.-2012.

6   "Crime in the United States 2017," U.S. Department of Justice, Federal Bureau of Investigation, Criminal Justice Information Services Division, Table 1, accessed October 29, 2018, https://ucr.fbi.gov/crime-in-the-u.s/2017/crime-in-the-u.s.-2017.

7   "Crime in the United States 2012," U.S. Department of Justice, Federal Bureau of Investigation, Criminal Justice Information Services Division, Table 1, accessed October 29, 2018, https://ucr.fbi.gov/crime-in-the-u.s/2012/crime-in-the-u.s.-2012.

8   "Crime in the United States 2017," U.S. Department of Justice, Federal Bureau of Investigation, Criminal Justice Information Services Division, Table 1, accessed October 29, 2018, https://ucr.fbi.gov/crime-in-the-u.s/2017/crime-in-the-u.s.-2017.

9   Niraj Chokshi, "California voters seem ready to end the state's 'tough on crime' era," *Washington Post*, October 31, 2014, https://www.washingtonpost.com/blogs/govbeat/wp/2014/10/31/california-voters-seem-ready-to-end-the-states-tough-on-crime-era/.

10   "John Blackstone, California goes from 'tough on crime' to 'let them go free,'" CBS News, November 27, 2014, https://www.cbsnews.com/news/california-goes-from-tough-on-crime-to-let-them-go-free/.

11   "Crime in California 2017," California Department of Justice, California Justice Information Services Division, Bureau of Criminal Information and Analysis, Criminal Justice Statistics Center, Table 1, July 9, 2018, https://openjustice.doj.ca.gov/downloads/pdfs/cd17.pdf.

12   Chris Kolmar, "These Are The Most Dangerous States In America For 2019," RoadSnacks, October 9, 2018, https://www.homesnacks.net/safest-states-in-america-127702/.

13   Chris Kolmar, "These Are The Most Dangerous Cities In America For 2019," RoadSnacks, October 29, 2018, https://www.roadsnacks.net/most-dangerous-cities/.

14   "Kevin Rizzo, America's Safest and Most Dangerous States 2017, Law Street Media, November 16, 2016, https://lawstreetmedia.com/blogs/crime/americas-safest-dangerous-states-2017/.

15   Michael B. Sauter, Thomas C. Frohlich, Evan Comen, "25 Most Dangerous Cities in America," 24/7 Wall St., January 19, 2018

16   "Crimes & Clearances 2007-2017, Los Angeles," Open Justice, California Department of Justice, accessed October 29, 2018, https://openjustice.doj.ca.gov/crime-statistics/crimes-clearances.

17   "Crimes & Clearances 2007-2017, Los Angeles," Open Justice, California Department of Justice, accessed October 29, 2018, https://openjustice.doj.ca.gov/crime-statistics/crimes-clearances.

18   Sean P. Thomas, "Number of Car Break-ins in Downtown Jumps by Nearly 30%," *Los Angeles Downtown News*, July 30, 2018, http://www.ladowntownnews.com/news/number-of-car-break-ins-in-downtown-jumps-by-nearly/article_df56c966-91e1-11e8-a306-6350f03ac902.html.

19   "Ben Poston, Joel Rubin, Anthony Pesce, LAPD underreported serious assaults, skewing crime stats for 8 years," *Los Angeles Times*, October 15, 2015, http://www.latimes.com/local/cityhall/la-me-crime-stats-20151015-story.html.

20   Ben Poston, Joel Rubin, Anthony Pesce, "LAPD underreported serious assaults, skewing crime stats for 8 years," *Los Angeles Times*, October 15, 2015, http://www.latimes.com/local/cityhall/la-me-crime-stats-20151015-story.html.

21   Matt Hamilton, "LAPD captain accuses department of twisting crime statistics to make city seem safer," *Los Angeles Times*, November 6, 2017, http://www.latimes.com/local/lanow/la-me-ln-lapd-crime-stats-claim-20171103-story.html.

22   Matt Hamilton, "LAPD captain accuses department of twisting crime statistics to make city seem safer," *Los Angeles Times*, November 6, 2017, http://www.latimes.com/local/lanow/la-me-ln-lapd-crime-stats-claim-20171103-story.html.

23   Matt Hamilton, "LAPD captain accuses department of twisting crime statistics to make city seem safer," *Los Angeles Times*, November 6, 2017, http://www.latimes.com/local/lanow/la-me-ln-lapd-crime-stats-claim-20171103-story.html.

24   Matt Hamilton, "LAPD captain accuses department of twisting crime statistics to make city seem safer," *Los Angeles Times*, November 6, 2017, http://www.latimes.com/local/lanow/la-me-ln-lapd-crime-stats-claim-20171103-story.html.

25   "Ben Poston, Joel Rubin, LAPD misclassified nearly 1,200 violent crimes as minor offenses," *Los Angeles Times*, August 9, 2014, http://www.latimes.com/local/la-me-crimestats-lapd-20140810-story.html.

26   Ben Poston, Joel Rubin, "LAPD misclassified nearly 1,200 violent crimes as minor offenses," *Los Angeles Times*, August 9, 2014, http://www.latimes.com/local/la-me-crimestats-lapd-20140810-story.html.

27   Ben Poston, Joel Rubin, "LAPD misclassified nearly 1,200 violent crimes as minor offenses," *Los Angeles Times*, August 9, 2014, http://www.latimes.com/local/la-me-crimestats-lapd-20140810-story.html.

28   "Valley LAPD captain says department under-reported violent crime stats despite her sounding alarm," *Los Angeles Daily News*, November 9, 2017, https://www.dailynews.com/2017/11/06/valley-lapd-captain-says-department-underreported-violent-crime-stats-despite-her-raising-concern/.

29   "Valley LAPD captain says department under-reported violent crime stats despite her sounding alarm," *Los Angeles Daily News*, November 9, 2017, https://www.dailynews.com/2017/11/06/valley-lapd-captain-says-department-underreported-violent-crime-stats-despite-her-raising-concern/.

30   "Crimes & Clearances 2007-2017, San Francisco," Open Justice, California Department of Justice, accessed October 29, 2018, https://openjustice.doj.ca.gov/crime-statistics/crimes-clearances.

31   Sarah Craig, "Car Break-Ins Are Up in San Francisco. What's Being Done?" KQED News, February 15, 2018, https://www.kqed.org/news/11643054/car-breaks-ins-are-up-in-san-francisco-whats-being-done.

32   Marc Debbaudt, "An explosion of California property crimes – due to Prop 47," *San Francisco Chronicle*, March 18, 2016, https://www.sfchronicle.com/opinion/openforum/article/An-explosion-of-California-property-crimes-6922062.php.

33   Bigad Shaban, Robert Campos, Anthony Rutanashoodech, "Hidden Cameras Reveal Rare View of 'Epidemic' as Car Break-Ins Hit Record High of Nearly 30,000 in San Francisco," KNTV-TV, February 25, 2018, https://www.nbcbayarea.com/news/local/Breaking-Point-475109113.html.

34   Evan Sernoffsky, "SF vehicle break-ins at record levels; police try new approach," *San Francisco Chronicle*, December 30, 2017, https://www.sfchronicle.com/crime/article/SF-vehicle-break-ins-at-record-levels-police-try-12464043.php.

35   Evan Sernoffsky, "SF vehicle break-ins at record levels; police try new approach," *San Francisco Chronicle*, December 30, 2017, https://www.sfchronicle.com/crime/article/SF-vehicle-break-ins-at-record-levels-police-try-12464043.php.

36   Sarah Craig, "Car Break-Ins Are Up in San Francisco. What's Being Done?" KQED News, February 15, 2018, https://www.kqed.org/news/11643054/car-breaks-ins-are-up-in-san-francisco-whats-being-done.

37   Sarah Craig, "Car Break-Ins Are Up in San Francisco. What's Being Done?" KQED News, February 15, 2018, https://www.kqed.org/news/11643054/car-breaks-ins-are-up-in-san-francisco-whats-being-done.

38   Michael Barba, "Gascon calls for task force to 'end' car break-in epidemic," *San Francisco Examiner*, February 21, 2018, http://www.sfexaminer.com/gascon-calls-task-force-end-car-break-epidemic/.

39   "Crimes & Clearances 2007-2017, San Diego," Open Justice, California Department of Justice, accessed October 29, 2018, https://openjustice.doj.ca.gov/crime-statistics/crimes-clearances.

40   Kristen Shanahan and City News Service, "3 people shot overnight in south San Diego," KSWB-TV, February 10, 2018, https://fox5sandiego.com/2018/02/10/3-people-shot-overnight-in-south-san-diego/.

41   "Police identify victim and suspect in murder that prompted weekend SWAT search," KSWB-TV, February 28, 2018, https://fox5sandiego.com/2018/02/28/victim-and-suspect-identified-in-murder-that-prompted-weekend-swat-search/.

42   Emily Shapiro, Karma Allen, "Suspected San Diego shooter 'had beer in one hand and his gun in the other,' witnesses say," ABC News, May 2, 2017, https://abcnews.go.com/US/woman-killed-people-injured-shooting-san-diego-apartment/story?id=47123185.

43   Lyndsay Winkley, "San Diego crime rate lowest in 49 years," *The San Diego Union-Tribune*, February 5, 2018, http://www.sandiegouniontribune.com/news/public-safety/sd-me-sandiego-crime-20180205-story.html.

44 Lyndsay Winkley, "San Diego crime rate lowest in 49 years," *The San Diego Union-Tribune*, February 5, 2018, http://www.sandiegouniontribune.com/news/public-safety/sd-me-sandiego-crime-20180205-story.html.

45 City News Service, "Crime rates show San Diego is safest big city for murders," September 25, 2017, https://www.10news.com/news/crime-rates-show-san-diego-is-safest-big-city-for-murders.

46 Lyndsay Winkley, "San Diego homicides drop sharply in past year but why?" *The San Diego Union-Tribune*, February 25, 2018, http://www.sandiegouniontribune.com/news/public-safety/sd-me-murder-statistics-20180221-story.html.

47 Lyndsay Winkley, "San Diego homicides drop sharply in past year but why?" *The San Diego Union-Tribune*, February 25, 2018, http://www.sandiegouniontribune.com/news/public-safety/sd-me-murder-statistics-20180221-story.html.

48 Lyndsay Winkley, "San Diego homicides drop sharply in past year but why?" *The San Diego Union-Tribune*, February 25, 2018, http://www.sandiegouniontribune.com/news/public-safety/sd-me-murder-statistics-20180221-story.html.

49 "ShotSpotter.com Frequently Asked Questions," ShotSpotter.com, January 2018, http://www.shotspotter.com/system/content-uploads/SST_FAQ_January_2018.pdf.

50 Lyndsay Winkley, "Is ShotSpotter helping combat gun violence, or just identifying it?" *The San Diego Union-Tribune*, December 18, 2017, http://www.sandiegouniontribune.com/news/public-safety/sd-me-annual-shotspotter-20171218-story.html.

51 Lyndsay Winkley, "Is ShotSpotter helping combat gun violence, or just identifying it?" *The San Diego Union-Tribune*, December 18, 2017, http://www.sandiegouniontribune.com/news/public-safety/sd-me-annual-shotspotter-20171218-story.html.

52 Dorian Hargrave, "Pacific Beach's high crime problem," *San Diego Reader*, February 12, 2018, https://www.sandiegoreader.com/news/2018/feb/12/ticker-pacific-beachs-high-crime-problem/#.

53 Dorian Hargrave, "Pacific Beach's high crime problem," *San Diego Reader*, February 12, 2018, https://www.sandiegoreader.com/news/2018/feb/12/ticker-pacific-beachs-high-crime-problem/#.

54 Monique Griego, "Pacific Beach residents want tougher punishments for crime," KFMB-TV, April 20, 2018, http://www.cbs8.com/story/38009160/pacific-beach-residents-want-tougher-punishments-for-crime.

55   Amber Lee, "Residents in Oakland's Montclair neighborhood concerned about an increase in crime," KTVU-TV, January 16, 2018, http://www.ktvu.com/news/residents-in-oaklands-montclair-neighborhood-concerned-about-an-increase-in-crime.

56   "Mayor Schaaf, OPD, Department of Violence Prevention and Community Address Steady Decline in Violent Crime," City of Oakland, January 9, 2018, https://www.oaklandca.gov/news/2018/mayor-schaaf-opd-department-of-violence-prevention-and-community-address-steady-decline-in-violent-crime.

57   Bay City News Service, "City Officials Announce 5-Year Reduction In Violent Crime," January 9, 2018, https://www.sfgate.com/news/bayarea/article/City-Officials-Announce-5-Year-Reduction-In-12486054.php.

58   Kimberly Veklerov, "Violent crime continues downward trend in Oakland, but car break-ins spike," *San Francisco Chronicle*, January 11, 2018, https://www.sfgate.com/crime/article/Violent-crime-continues-downward-trend-in-12489042.php.

59   Kimberly Veklerov, "Violent crime continues downward trend in Oakland, but car break-ins spike," *San Francisco Chronicle*, January 11, 2018, https://www.sfgate.com/crime/article/Violent-crime-continues-downward-trend-in-12489042.php.

60   "Oakland's Ceasefire Strategy," City of Oakland, Police Department, accessed October 29, 2018, https://www.oaklandca.gov/topics/oaklands-ceasefire-strategy.

61   Kimberly Veklerov, "Violent crime continues downward trend in Oakland, but car break-ins spike," *San Francisco Chronicle*, January 11, 2018, https://www.sfgate.com/crime/article/Violent-crime-continues-downward-trend-in-12489042.php.

62   Amber Lee, "Residents in Oakland's Montclair neighborhood concerned about an increase in crime," KTVU-TV, January 16, 2018, http://www.ktvu.com/news/residents-in-oaklands-montclair-neighborhood-concerned-about-an-increase-in-crime.

63   Amber Lee, "Residents in Oakland's Montclair neighborhood concerned about an increase in crime," KTVU-TV, January 16, 2018, http://www.ktvu.com/news/residents-in-oaklands-montclair-neighborhood-concerned-about-an-increase-in-crime.

64   Juliette Goodrich, "Oakland Supermarket Clerk Fired For Trying To Stop Shoplifter," KPIX-TV, January 15, 2018, https://sanfrancisco.cbslocal.com/2018/01/15/lucky-supermarket-clerk-fired-shoplifter/.

65   Amber Lee, "Residents in Oakland's Montclair neighborhood concerned about an increase in crime," KTVU-TV, January 16, 2018, http://www.ktvu.com/news/residents-in-oaklands-montclair-neighborhood-concerned-about-an-increase-in-crime.

66   Nashelly Chavez, "Crime drops again in Sacramento – here's why, according to police and residents," *Sacramento Bee*, February 10, 2018, https://www.sacbee.com/news/local/article199389254.html.

67   Nashelly Chavez, "Crime drops again in Sacramento – here's why, according to police and residents," *Sacramento Bee*, February 10, 2018, https://www.sacbee.com/news/local/article199389254.html.

68   Nashelly Chavez, "Crime drops again in Sacramento – here's why, according to police and residents," *Sacramento Bee*, February 10, 2018, https://www.sacbee.com/news/local/article199389254.html.

69   Michelle Perin, "Engage in Social Media for Overall Crime Prevention," Officer.com, November 16, 2017, https://www.officer.com/command-hq/technology/article/20978573/engage-in-social-media-for-overall-crime-prevention.

70   Michelle Perin, "Engage in Social Media for Overall Crime Prevention," Officer.com, November 16, 2017, https://www.officer.com/command-hq/technology/article/20978573/engage-in-social-media-for-overall-crime-prevention.

71   Katrina Cameron, "Sacramento police tout NextDoor social media site for fighting crime," *Sacramento Bee*, October 8, 2014, https://www.sacbee.com/news/local/crime/article2602387.html.

72   Robert Salonga, "San Jose leads array of California cities with spiking violent crime," *Mercury News*, December 30, 2017, https://www.mercurynews.com/2017/12/30/san-jose-leads-array-of-california-cities-with-spiking-violent-crime/.

73   Robert Salonga, "San Jose leads array of California cities with spiking violent crime," *Mercury News*, December 30, 2017, https://www.mercurynews.com/2017/12/30/san-jose-leads-array-of-california-cities-with-spiking-violent-crime/.

74   Robert Salonga, "San Jose: Arrest of adult-teen robbery crew highlights new wave of 'gang' crimes," *Mercury News*, January 18, 2018, https://www.mercurynews.com/2018/01/16/san-jose-arrest-of-adult-teen-robbery-crew-highlights-new-wave-of-gang-crimes/.

75   Jared Gilmour, "With an 11-year-old getaway driver, they robbed and carjacked 15 victims at gunpoint, police say," *Sacramento Bee*, November 29, 2017, https://www.modbee.com/news/article187229428.html.

76   Jared Gilmour, "With an 11-year-old getaway driver, they robbed and carjacked 15 victims at gunpoint, police say," *Sacramento Bee*, November 29, 2017, https://www.modbee.com/news/article187229428.html.

77   Editorial Board, "Editorial: Crime in Oakland goes down, rises in San Jose — what's up with that?" *Mercury News*, January 21, 2018, https://www.mercurynews.com/2018/01/13/editorial-crime-in-oakland-goes-down-rises-in-san-jose-whats-up-with-that/.

78   "FBI Report: Crime Continues To Increase In California Cities," Criminal Justice Legal Foundation, January 25, 2018, https://www.cjlf.org/releases/18-01.htm.

79   "FBI Report: Crime Continues To Increase In California Cities," Criminal Justice Legal Foundation, January 25, 2018, https://www.cjlf.org/releases/18-01.htm.

80   Andy Nguyen, "Violent offenses rose in Glendale for 2017, while overall crime rate declined," *Los Angeles Times-Glendale News-Press*, February 6, 2018

81   Andy Nguyen, "While overall crime rate dips in Glendale, stats show a rise in violent offenses," *Los Angeles Times-Glendale News-Press*, February 24, 2017

82   Paola Baker, "Never-ending battle," *Victorville Daily Press*, April 24, 2018

83   Josh Cain, "Dozens of Los Angeles-area gang members arrested in major FBI raid targeting Mexican Mafia," *Los Angeles Daily News*, May 23, 2018

84   Emilie Raguso, "Violent crime is up again in Berkeley," *Berkeleyside*, March 19, 2018, https://www.berkeleyside.com/2018/03/19/violent-crime-berkeley.

85   Billy O'Connell, "It's time to stop playing politics and declare war on crime in Huntington Beach," *Los Angeles Times*, March 5, 2018, http://www.latimes.com/socal/daily-pilot/opinion/tn-dpt-me-commentary-hb-20180305-story.html.

86   "The Safest and Most Dangerous Cities in the U.S.," *Insurance Journal*, May 8, 2018, https://www.insurancejournal.com/news/national/2018/05/08/488586.htm.

87   "Crimes & Clearances 2007-2016, Stockton," California Department of Justice, accessed October 29, 2018, https://openjustice.doj.ca.gov/crime-statistics/crimes-clearances.

88   Steve Lopez, "Stockton's young mayor has bold turnaround plan: Basic income and stipends for potential shooters," *Los Angeles Times*, May 26, 2018, http://www.latimes.com/local/california/la-me-lopez-stockton-money-05272018-story.html.

89   Steve Lopez, "Stockton's young mayor has bold turnaround plan: Basic income and stipends for potential shooters," *Los Angeles Times*, May 26, 2018, http://www.latimes.com/local/california/la-me-lopez-stockton-money-05272018-story.html.

90   Jeremy Thomas, "The rural jurisdiction," *Santa Maria Sun*, September 26, 2012, http://www.santamariasun.com/cover/8792/the-rural-jurisdiction/.

91   Jeremy Thomas, "The rural jurisdiction," *Santa Maria Sun*, September 26, 2012, http://www.santamariasun.com/cover/8792/the-rural-jurisdiction/.

92   California Farm Bureau, Top Issues, Rural Crime Prevention, Metal Theft

93   Noelle G. Cremers, e-mail message to author, April 30, 2018.

94   Noelle G. Cremers, e-mail message to author, April 30, 2018.

95   Victor Davis Hanson, "A Vandalized Valley," *National Review*, December 21, 2011

96   Victor Davis Hanson, "A Vandalized Valley," *National Review*, December 21, 2011

97   Victor Davis Hanson, e-mail message to author, April 23, 2018.

98   Taylor Roschen, e-mail message to author, April 30, 2018.

99   Taylor Roschen, e-mail message to author, April 30, 2018.

100   City News Service, "Gang member shot to death in Bell Gardens," January 5, 2018, https://www.ocregister.com/2018/01/05/gang-member-shot-to-death-in-bell-gardens/.

101   City News Service, "Gang member killed by shot to the head in South LA," August 28, 2017, https://www.dailynews.com/2017/07/20/gang-member-killed-by-shot-to-the-head-in-south-la/.

102   Larry Altman, "Palos Verdes High senior charged in South LA gang killing," *Daily Breeze*, November 10, 2017, https://www.dailybreeze.com/2017/11/09/palos-verdes-high-senior-charged-in-south-los-angeles-gang-killing/.

103   "Gangs," Los Angeles Policy Department, accessed October 29, 2018, http://www.lapdonline.org/get_informed/content_basic_view/1396.

104   "Gang-Related Crime Los Angeles County," Los Angeles Almanac, accessed October 29, 2018, http://www.laalmanac.com/crime/cr03x.php.

105   "Gang Statistics By Month Archived," Los Angeles Police Department, accessed October 29, 2018, http://www.lapdonline.org/get_informed/content_basic_view/24435.

106   Cindy Chang, "LAPD analysis shows homicide victims are overwhelmingly young, nonwhite and poor," *Los Angeles Times*, January 31, 2018, http://www.latimes.com/local/lanow/la-me-lapd-homicides-20180131-story.html.

107   City News Service, "Gang-related, domestic violence crimes spike in Los Angeles," January 13, 2016, https://www.dailynews.com/2016/01/13/gang-related-domestic-violence-crimes-spike-in-los-angeles/.

108   City News Service, "Gang-related, domestic violence crimes spike in Los Angeles," January 13, 2016, https://www.dailynews.com/2016/01/13/gang-related-domestic-violence-crimes-spike-in-los-angeles/.

109   "What You Need To Know About Gangs In Los Angeles In 2015 ~ A Q&A With Sam Quinones," *L.A. Taco*, February 23, 2015, https://www.lataco.com/gangs-los-angeles-2015-sam-quinones/.

110   "What You Need To Know About Gangs In Los Angeles In 2015 ~ A Q&A With Sam Quinones," *L.A. Taco*, February 23, 2015, https://www.lataco.com/gangs-los-angeles-2015-sam-quinones/.

111   Sam Quinones, "A change in the landscape: L.A.'s parks no longer belong to street gangs," *Los Angeles Times*, February 7, 2015, http://www.latimes.com/opinion/op-ed/la-oe-0208-quinones-parks-gangs-20150208-story.html.

112   Sam Quinones, "LAPD Chief Charlie Beck and What Really Matters," Dreamland … a Reporter's Blog from author/journalist Sam Quinones, January 24, 2018, http://samquinones.com/reporters-blog/2018/01/24/lapd-chief-charlie-beck-really-matters/.

113   Sam Quinones, "LAPD Chief Charlie Beck and What Really Matters," Dreamland … a Reporter's Blog from author/journalist Sam Quinones, January 24, 2018, http://samquinones.com/reporters-blog/2018/01/24/lapd-chief-charlie-beck-really-matters/.

114   "Gang Injunctions," Los Angeles Policy Department, accessed October 29, 2018, http://www.lapdonline.org/gang_injunctions.

115   Editorial Board, "Keeping gang injunctions in L.A.'s crime-fighting toolbox," *Los Angeles Times*, March 20, 2018.

116   Matthew D. O'Deane, Stephen A. Morreale, "Evaluation of the Effectiveness of Gang Injunctions in California," *The Journal of Criminal Justice Research* 2, no. 1 (2011), http://www.academia.edu/970697/Evaluation_of_the_Effectiveness_of_Gang_Injunctions_in_California.

117   City News Service, "Federal Judge Bars City of LA From Enforcing Gang Injunctions," March 16, 2018, https://www.nbclosangeles.com/news/local/federal-judge-Thursday-barred-city-Los-Angeles-enforcing-gang-injunctions-477134173.html.

118   Editorial Board, "Keep gang injunctions in L.A.'s crime-fighthing box," *Los Angeles Times*, March 20, 2018.

119   Editorial Board "Keep gang injunctions in L.A.'s crime-fighthing box," , *Los Angeles Times*, March 20, 2018.

120   Denisse Salazar, "With 13,000 gang members in Orange County, the push is on to curb crime and recruitment," *Orange County Register*, November 8, 2017, https://www.ocregister.com/2017/11/07/with-13000-gang-members-in-o-c-the-push-is-on-to-break-the-cycle/.

121   Denisse Salazar, "With 13,000 gang members in Orange County, the push is on to curb crime and recruitment," *Orange County Register*, November 8, 2017, https://www.ocregister.com/2017/11/07/with-13000-gang-members-in-o-c-the-push-is-on-to-break-the-cycle/.

122   Jim Bueermann, "OCGRIP is a national model for preventing gang membership," *Orange County Register*, February 2, 2018, https://www.ocregister.com/2018/02/02/ocgrip-is-a-national-model-for-preventing-gang-membership/.

123   Jim Bueermann, "OCGRIP is a national model for preventing gang membership," *Orange County Register*, February 2, 2018, https://www.ocregister.com/2018/02/02/ocgrip-is-a-national-model-for-preventing-gang-membership/.

124   Leo Smith, "Thanksgiving meals ready for Orange County kids who passed gang prevention challenge," *Orange County Register*, November 14, 2017, https://www.ocregister.com/2017/11/14/thanksgiving-meals-ready-for-orange-county-kids-who-passed-gang-prevention-challenge/.

125   Denisse Salazar, "With 13,000 gang members in Orange County, the push is on to curb crime and recruitment," *Orange County Register*, November 8, 2017, https://www.ocregister.com/2017/11/07/with-13000-gang-members-in-o-c-the-push-is-on-to-break-the-cycle/.

126   Denisse Salazar, "With 13,000 gang members in Orange County, the push is on to curb crime and recruitment," *Orange County Register*, November 8, 2017, https://www.ocregister.com/2017/11/07/with-13000-gang-members-in-o-c-the-push-is-on-to-break-the-cycle/.

127   Denisse Salazar, "With 13,000 gang members in Orange County, the push is on to curb crime and recruitment," *Orange County Register*, November 8, 2017, https://www.ocregister.com/2017/11/07/with-13000-gang-members-in-o-c-the-push-is-on-to-break-the-cycle/.

128   Jessica Peralta, "Orange County GRIP three-day soccer camp helps at-risk youth choose right over wrong," *Behind the Badge*, April 28, 2017, http://behindthebadge.com/cities/fpd/orange-county-grip-3-day-soccer-camp-helps-keep-risk-kids-gangs.

129   Greg Lee, "OC Officials crack down on curfew violators to help keep minors out of trouble," KABC-TV, March 31, 2016, https://abc7.com/news/crackdown-on-orange-county-teens-out-after-curfew/1931148/.

130   David Ropeik, "School shootings are extraordinarily rare. Why is fear of them driving policy?" *The Washington Post*, March 8, 2018, https://www.washingtonpost.com/outlook/school-shootings-are-extraordinarily-rare-why-is-fear-of-them-driving-policy/2018/03/08/f4ead9f2-2247-11e8-94da-ebf9d112159c_story.html?utm_term=.5659bc667a56.

131 Data show that shooting incidents involving students have been falling since the 1990s. Allie Nicodemo, Lia Petronio, "Schools are safer than they were in the 90s, and school shootings are not more common than they used to be, researchers say," *News @ Northeastern*, Northeastern University, February 26, 2018, https://news.northeastern.edu/2018/02/26/schools-are-still-one-of-the-safest-places-for-children-researcher-says/.

132 Journalist Eric Levitz says "an American's lifetime odds of dying in a mass shooting committed in any location is 1 in 11,125; of dying in a car accident is 1 and 491; of drowning is 1 in 1,133; and of choking on food is 1 in 3,461." Eric Levitz, "There Is No 'Epidemic of Mass School Shootings,'" *New York Magazine*, March 1, 2018, http://nymag.com/intelligencer/2018/03/there-is-no-epidemic-of-mass-school-shootings.html?gtm=bottom&gtm=bottom.

133 "Indicators of School Crime and Safety: 2017," National Center for Education Statistics, U.S. Department of Education, March 2018, https://nces.ed.gov/pubs2018/2018036.pdf.

134 "Indicators of School Crime and Safety: 2016," National Center for Education Statistics, U.S. Department of Education, May 2017, https://nces.ed.gov/pubs2017/2017064.pdf.

135 "Indicators of School Crime and Safety: 2017," National Center for Education Statistics, U.S. Department of Education, March 2018, https://nces.ed.gov/pubs2018/2018036.pdf.

136 "Indicators of School Crime and Safety: 2014," National Center for Education Statistics, U.S. Department of Education, July 2015, https://nces.ed.gov/pubsearch/pubsinfo.asp?pubid=2015072.

137 "Indicators of School Crime and Safety: 2009," National Center for Education Statistics, U.S. Department of Education, December 2009, https://nces.ed.gov/pubsearch/pubsinfo.asp?pubid=2010012.

138 "Indicators of School Crime and Safety: 2016," National Center for Education Statistics, U.S. Department of Education, May 2017, https://nces.ed.gov/pubs2017/2017064.pdf.

139 "Indicators of School Crime and Safety: 2014," National Center for Education Statistics, U.S. Department of Education, July 2015, https://nces.ed.gov/pubsearch/pubsinfo.asp?pubid=2015072.

140 "Indicators of School Crime and Safety: 2009," National Center for Education Statistics, U.S. Department of Education, December 2009, https://nces.ed.gov/pubsearch/pubsinfo.asp?pubid=2010012.

141 Lance Izumi, telephone interview with author, March 23, 2018

142 Rory Appleton, "Bullard High student allegedly attacks teacher, student; campus police officer slow to respond," *Fresno Bee*, November 21, 2015, https://www.fresnobee.com/news/local/crime/article45632931.html.

143 Rory Appleton, "Roosevelt High student arrested after videos show her punching teacher," *Fresno Bee*, September 11, 2015, https://www.fresnobee.com/news/local/crime/article34613712.html.

144 "Roosevelt High girls arrested after attack on student," *Fresno Bee*, October 1, 2015, https://www.fresnobee.com/news/local/crime/article37111467.html.

145 Veronica Rocha, "Cellphone videos show massive lunchtime brawl at Sylmar High School," *Los Angeles Times*, May 10, 2016, http://www.latimes.com/local/lanow/la-me-ln-massive-brawl-sylmar-high-school-20160510-story.html.

146 "Viral video captures violent California school assault," KABC-TV, November 14, 2017, https://abc7ny.com/viral-video-captures-violent-school-assault/2646444/.

147 Editorial Board, "Thugs Run L.A. Classrooms, Thanks To Obama Suspension Plan," *Investor's Business Daily*, July 2, 2014.

148 Lyanne Menendez, "Protest held in San Francisco against policy allowing violent kids to stay in class," KGO San Francisco, May 24, 2016, https://abc7news.com/education/protest-held-in-sf-against-policy-allowing-violent-kids-to-stay-in-class/1353731/.

149 Sarah Favot, "Pasadena school board eliminates suspensions for 'willful defiance,'" *Pasadena Star-News*, August 28, 2017, https://www.pasadenastarnews.com/2014/12/26/pasadena-school-board-eliminates-suspensions-for-willful-defiance/.

150 Susan Frey, "Oakland ends suspensions for willful defiance, funds restorative justice," *EdSource*, May 14, 2015, https://edsource.org/2015/oakland-ends-suspensions-for-willful-defiance-funds-restorative-justice/79731.

151 David Washburn, "Gov. Brown vetoes expansion of California's school suspension ban," *EdSource*, October 1, 2018, https://edsource.org/2018/gov-brown-vetoes-expansion-of-californias-school-suspension-ban/603084.

152 David Griffith, e-mail message to author, April 2, 2018.

153 Lance Izumi, *The Corrupt Classroom* (San Francisco: Pacific Research Institute, June 2017), 44.

154 Lance Izumi, *The Corrupt Classroom* (San Francisco: Pacific Research Institute, June 2017), 44.

155 Max Eden, "California putting vulnerable students in harm's way," *Orange County Register*, May 22, 2017, https://www.ocregister.com/2017/05/21/california-putting-vulnerable-students-in-harms-way/.

156 Max Eden, "California putting vulnerable students in harm's way," *Orange County Register*, May 22, 2017, https://www.ocregister.com/2017/05/21/california-putting-vulnerable-students-in-harms-way/.

157 Max Eden, "California putting vulnerable students in harm's way," *Orange County Register*, May 22, 2017, https://www.ocregister.com/2017/05/21/california-putting-vulnerable-students-in-harms-way/.

158 Matthew P. Steinberg, Johanna Lace, "The Academic and Behavioral Consequences of Discipline Policy Reform," Thomas B. Fordham Institute, December 2017, https://edexcellence.net/publications/discipline-reform-philadelphia.

159 David Griffith, "Discipline mandates are unlikely to fix tough schools' underlying issues," Thomas B. Fordham Institute, December 5, 2017, https://edexcellence.net/articles/discipline-mandates-are-unlikely-to-fix-tough-schools-underlying-issues.

160 Lance Izumi, *The Corrupt Classroom* (San Francisco: Pacific Research Institute, June 2017), 47.

161 Scott Carrell and Mark Hoekstra, "Domino Effect," *EducationNext* 9, No. 3 (Summer 2009).

162 Scott Carrell and Mark Hoekstra, "Domino Effect," *EducationNext* 9, No. 3 (Summer 2009).

163 Lance Izumi, *The Corrupt Classroom* (San Francisco: Pacific Research Institute, June 2017), 48.

164 Lance Izumi, *The Corrupt Classroom* (San Francisco: Pacific Research Institute, June 2017), 49.

165 Lance Izumi, telephone interview with author, March 23, 2018.

166 Lance Izumi, telephone interview with author, March 23, 2018.

167 Claudia Detotto, Edoardo Otranto, "Does Crime Affect Economic Growth?" *Kyklos* 63, no. 3, pages 330-345, (August 2010), https://onlinelibrary.wiley.com/doi/abs/10.1111/j.1467-6435.2010.00477.x.

168 Paul Heaton, "In Broad Daylight: New Crime Calculator Brings Crime Costs – and the Value of Police – Out of the Shadows," Rand Corporation, Spring 2012, https://www.rand.org/pubs/infographics/IG105.html.

169 Paul Heaton, "Hidden in Plain Sight: What Cost-of-Crime Research Can Tell Us About Investing in Police," Rand Corporation, 2010, https://www.rand.org/pubs/occasional_papers/OP279.html.

170 Abbie Alford, "Imperial Beach parking lot closed due to recent crime," KFMB-TV, September 6, 2015, http://www.cbs8.com/story/29965161/imperial-beach-parking-lot-closed-due-to-recent-crime.

171 Jim Hilborn, "Problem-Oriented Guides for Police, Response Guides Series No. 9: Dealing With Crime and Disorder in Urban Parks," U.S. Department of Justice, Office of Community Oriented Policing Services, May 2009, http://www.popcenter.org/responses/PDFs/urban_parks.pdf.

172 Marjie Lundstrom, Matt Weiser, "Rising crime dims luster of California state parks," *Sacramento Bee*, October 6, 2014, https://www.sacbee.com/news/investigations/state-parks-funding/article2572950.html.

173 Paul T. Rosynsky, "Cop killer gets death sentence," *East Bay Times*, August 17, 2017, https://www.eastbaytimes.com/2007/06/12/cop-killer-gets-death-sentence-2/.

174 "California Crime Victims' Voices: Findings from the First-Ever Survey of California Crime Victims and Survivors," Californians for Safety and Justice, accessed October 29, 2018, https://safeandjust.org/wp-content/uploads/CA-Crime-Victims-Report-8_24_17.pdf.

175 Heather Warnken, Esq., LL.M., "Untold Stories Of California Crime Victims: Research and Recommendations of Repeat Victimization and Rebuilding Lives," Berkeley Law, Chief Justice Earl Warren Institute on Law and Social Policy, April 2014, https://www.law.berkeley.edu/files/WI_CA_Untold_Stories_03_31_14_lo_res_Final.pdf.

176 Jens Ludwig, "The costs of crime," *Criminology & Public Policy* 9, no. 2, (2010),

177 "Economics And Social Effects Of Crime," *Crime and Punishment in America Reference Library*, Encyclopedia.com, October 17, 2018, https://www.encyclopedia.com/law/encyclopedias-almanacs-transcripts-and-maps/economic-and-social-effects-crime.

178 Richard Florida, "Violent Crime's Toll on Economic Mobility," *CityLab.com*, August 22, 2017, https://www.citylab.com/equity/2017/08/violent-crimes-toll-on-economic-mobility/537549/.

179 "Health Effects of Gentrification," Centers for Disease Control and Prevention, October 15, 2009, https://www.cdc.gov/healthyplaces/healthtopics/gentrification.htm.

180 Rebecca Linke, "Gentrification triggers 16 percent drop in city crime in Cambridge, Massachusetts," *Phys.org*, December 27, 2017, https://phys.org/news/2017-12-gentrification-triggers-percent-city-crime.html/

181 Rebecca Linke, "Gentrification triggers 16 percent drop in city crime in Cambridge, Massachusetts," *Phys.org*, December 27, 2017, https://phys.org/news/2017-12-gentrification-triggers-percent-city-crime.html.

182 Ronald L. Simons, Callie Harbin Burt, "Learning To Be Bad: Adverse Social Conditions, Social Schemas, And Crime," *Criminology* 49, no. 2 (May 2011), https://www.ncbi.nlm.nih.gov/pmc/articles/PMC3134330/.

183 "2017 Gun Law State Scorecard," Giffords Law Center to Prevent Gun Violence, accessed October 29, 2018, https://lawcenter.giffords.org/scorecard/.

184 Jeff Asher, Mai Nguyen, "Gun Laws Stop At State Lines, But Guns Don't," *FiveThirtyEight*, October 26, 2017, https://fivethirtyeight.com/features/gun-laws-stop-at-state-lines-but-guns-dont/.

185 "Gun Violence Statistics by State," DemographicData.org, accessed October 29, 2018, http://demographicdata.org/crime-rates/gun-violence-statistics-by-state/.

186 "Crime in California 2016," California Department of Justice, California Justice Information Services Division, Bureau of Criminal Information and Analysis, Criminal Justice Statistics Center, Table 4, accessed October 29, 2018, https://openjustice.doj.ca.gov/downloads/pdfs/cd16.pdf.

187 "Crime in California 2017," California Department of Justice, California Justice Information Services Division, Bureau of Criminal Information and Analysis, Criminal Justice Statistics Center, Table 4, July 9, 2018, https://openjustice.doj.ca.gov/downloads/pdfs/cd17.pdf.

188 "Crime in California 2017," California Department of Justice, California Justice Information Services Division, Bureau of Criminal Information and Analysis, Criminal Justice Statistics Center, Table 4, July 9, 2018, https://openjustice.doj.ca.gov/downloads/pdfs/cd17.pdf.

189 Patrick May, Robert Salonga, "California's unique gun confiscation program in spotlight after Texas church massacre," *East Bay Times,* November 17, 2017, https://www.eastbaytimes.com/2017/11/07/californias-unique-gun-confiscation-program-in-spotlight-after-texas-church-massacre/.

190 "Bureau of Firearms," California Department of Justice, accessed October 29, 2018, https://oag.ca.gov/careers/descriptions/firearms.

191 Patrick McGreevy, "10,000 Californians barred from owning guns are still armed. This law aims to change that," *Los Angeles Times*, January 19, 2018, http://www.latimes.com/politics/la-pol-ca-gun-seizures-felons-20180119-story.html.

192 "Budget Subcommittee Spotlight," California State Senate Republican Caucus, April 19, 2018.

193 "Budget Subcommittee Spotlight," California State Senate Republican Caucus, April 19, 2018.

194 "Budget Subcommittee Spotlight," California State Senate Republican Caucus, April 19, 2018.

195 "Armed and Prohibited Persons System, SB 140 Legislative Report Number Four, Calendar Year 2017," Office of the California Attorney General, March 9, 2018, https://oag.ca.gov/sites/all/files/agweb/pdfs/publications/armed-prohib-person-system-2017.pdf.

196 California Senate Republican Caucus, Letter to California Attorney General Xavier Becerra, April 3, 2018.

197   California Senate Republican Caucus, Letter to California Attorney General Xavier Becerra, April 3, 2018.

198   California Senate Republican Caucus, Letter to California Attorney General Xavier Becerra, April 3, 2018.

199   Steven Greenhut, "Losing Their Gun Rights With Barely a Whimper," *The American Spectator*, July 13, 2017, https://spectator.org/losing-their-gun-rights-with-barely-a-whimper/.

200   Angela Greenwood, "Eyewitness News Investigates: Flaws Within California's Gun Confiscation Program," KSEE-TV and KGPE-TV, February, 8, 2016, https://www.yourcentralvalley.com/news/eyewitness-news-investigates-flaws-within-californias-gun-confiscation-program/358532978.

201   Angela Greenwood, "Eyewitness News Investigates: Flaws Within California's Gun Confiscation Program," KSEE-TV and KGPE-TV, February, 8, 2016, https://www.yourcentralvalley.com/news/eyewitness-news-investigates-flaws-within-californias-gun-confiscation-program/358532978.

202   Angela Greenwood, "Eyewitness News Investigates: Flaws Within California's Gun Confiscation Program," KSEE-TV and KGPE-TV, February, 8, 2016, https://www.yourcentralvalley.com/news/eyewitness-news-investigates-flaws-within-californias-gun-confiscation-program/358532978.

203   "California's Armed & Prohibited Persons Program Being Credited For Recent Arrest Is Dubious," *Ammoland*, July 5, 2013, https://www.ammoland.com/2013/07/californias-armed-prohibited-persons-program-being-credited-for-recent-arrest-is-dubious/#axzz5VROxLYDI.

204   "CDCR Releases Back-to-Back Annual Recidivism Reports," California Department of Corrections and Rehabilitation, October 10, 2017, https://news.cdcr.ca.gov/news-releases/2017/10/10/cdcr-releases-back-to-back-annual-recidivism-reports/.

205   "CDCR Releases Back-to-Back Annual Recidivism Reports," California Department of Corrections and Rehabilitation, October 10, 2017, https://news.cdcr.ca.gov/news-releases/2017/10/10/cdcr-releases-back-to-back-annual-recidivism-reports/.

206   Associated Press, "California Counties Looking To Cut Down On Re-Offenders In Realignment," August 25, 2013, https://sacramento.cbslocal.com/2013/08/25/california-counties-looking-to-cut-down-on-re-offenders-in-realignment/.

207   Dan Walters, "New definition of recidivism minimizes political fallout from prison realignment," *Sacramento Bee*, September 29, 2014.

208   "Improving In-Prison Rehabilitation Programs," California Legislative Analyst's Office, December 6, 2017, https://lao.ca.gov/Publications/Report/3720.

209   "Improving In-Prison Rehabilitation Programs," California Legislative Analyst's Office, December 6, 2017, https://lao.ca.gov/Publications/Report/3720.

210   "Improving In-Prison Rehabilitation Programs," California Legislative Analyst's Office, December 6, 2017, https://lao.ca.gov/Publications/Report/3720.

211   "Improving In-Prison Rehabilitation Programs," California Legislative Analyst's Office, December 6, 2017, https://lao.ca.gov/Publications/Report/3720.

212   "Improving In-Prison Rehabilitation Programs," California Legislative Analyst's Office, December 6, 2017, https://lao.ca.gov/Publications/Report/3720.

213   Juan Haines, "Code.7370 Certifies 12 Men As Web App Developers," *San Quentin News*, May 1, 2015, https://sanquentinnews.com/code-7370-certifies-12-men-as-web-app-developers/.

214   Juan Haines, "Code.7370 Certifies 12 Men As Web App Developers," *San Quentin News*, May 1, 2015, https://sanquentinnews.com/code-7370-certifies-12-men-as-web-app-developers/.

215   Michael Newberg, "A non-profit is helping ex-convicts land jobs as Silicon Valley programmers," CNBC, December 11, 2017, https://uk.finance.yahoo.com/news/non-profit-helping-ex-convicts-140000458.html.

216   "Report To The Legislature: Fiscal Year 2016-17," California Prison Industry Authority, February 1, 2018, https://www.calpia.ca.gov/news/reports-and-publications/report-to-the-legislature-fiscal-year-2016-17/.

217   Michael Newberg, "Convicts at San Quentin State Prison are learning to code – and some land jobs in tech when they get out," CNBC, April 11, 2017, https://www.cnbc.com/2017/04/10/san-quentin-inmate-coding-program-the-last-mile.html.

218   "Jesuit founder of L.A. gang rehabilitation program to speak at Mystical Rose Oratory," *Hawaii Catholic Herald*, February 8, 2018, http://www.hawaiicatholicherald.com/2018/02/08/jesuit-founder-of-l-a-gang-rehabilitation-program-to-speak-at-mystical-rose-oratory/.

219   Paolo, "Food Awards, Part I: The Bon Appetit Awards," *Eater San Francisco*, September 19, 2007, https://sf.eater.com/2007/9/19/6812925/food-awards-part-i-the-bon-appetit-awards.

220   Amanda Skofstad, "Rev. Gregory J. Boyle, S.J., founder of Homeboy Industries, to receive Notre Dame's 2017 Laetare Medal," *Notre Dame News*, March 26, 2017, https://news.nd.edu/news/rev-gregory-j-boyle-sj-founder-of-homeboy-industries-to-receive-notre-dames-2017-laetare-medal/.

221   Will Lopez, "I've Had My Second Chance Here – And My Third, And My Fourth," Transformation Stories, Homeboy Industries, accessed October 29, 2018, https://www.homeboyindustries.org/site/transformation_stories/P9.

222   Will Lopez, "I've Had My Second Chance Here – And My Third, And My Fourth," Transformation Stories, Homeboy Industries, accessed October 29, 2018, https://www.homeboyindustries.org/site/transformation_stories/P9.

223   Will Lopez, "I've Had My Second Chance Here – And My Third, And My Fourth," Transformation Stories, Homeboy Industries, accessed October 29, 2018, https://www.homeboyindustries.org/site/transformation_stories/P9.

224   Michaela Shea, "Jose Osuna: A Homeboy Finds A Seat At The Table," *National Jesuit News*, May 16, 2017, http://www.jesuits.org/story?TN=PROJECT-20170515010710.

225   Michaela Shea, "Jose Osuna: A Homeboy Finds A Seat At The Table," *National Jesuit News*, May 16, 2017, http://www.jesuits.org/story?TN=PROJECT-20170515010710/.

226   Austill Stuart, "Private prisons are helping California and can be used to reduce prison population," *The Orange County Register*, April 10, 2017, https://www.ocregister.com/2017/03/31/private-prisons-are-helping-california-and-can-be-used-to-reduce-prison-population/.

227   Hon. J. Richard Couzens and Hon. Tricia A. Bigelow, "The Amendment Of The Three Strikes Sentencing Law," Barrister Press, May 2017, http://www.courts.ca.gov/documents/Three-Strikes-Amendment-Couzens-Bigelow.pdf.

228   Hon. J. Richard Couzens and Hon. Tricia A. Bigelow, "The Amendment Of The Three Strikes Sentencing Law," Barrister Press, May 2017, http://www.courts.ca.gov/documents/Three-Strikes-Amendment-Couzens-Bigelow.pdf.

229   Maura Dolan, "California Supreme Court makes it harder for three-strike prisoners to get sentence reductions," *Los Angeles Times*, July 3, 2017, http://www.latimes.com/local/lanow/la-me-ln-three-strikes-court-20170703-story.html.

230   Ryken Grattet, "Sentence Enhancements: Next Targets of Corrections Reform?" Public Policy Institute of California, September 27, 2017, http://www.ppic.org/blog/sentence-enhancements-next-target-corrections-reform/.

231   Tomislav V. Kovandzic, John J. Sloan III, and Lynne M. Vieraitis, "'Striking out' as crime reduction policy: The impact of 'three strikes' laws on crime rates in U.S. Cities," *Justice Quarterly* 21, no. 2 (June 2004): 207-239.

232   Tomislav V. Kovandzic, John J. Sloan III, and Lynne M. Vieraitis, "'Striking out' as crime reduction policy: The impact of 'three strikes' laws on crime rates in U.S. Cities," *Justice Quarterly* 21, no. 2 (June 2004): 207-239.

233   Pablo Lopez, "Ex-con fessed up to the gun charge. But the sentence left the judge and DA feuding," *Fresno Bee*, October 24, 2017, https://www.fresnobee.com/news/local/crime/article180722181.html

234 "California Changes to Three-Strikes Sentencing Law and Prison Savings Allocation Initiative (2018)," Ballotpedia, accessed October 29, 2018, https://ballotpedia.org/California_Changes_to_Three-Strikes_Sentencing_Law_and_Prison_Savings_Allocation_Initiative_(2018).

235 "California Realignment: LA Shootings May Be Linked To Inmates Released On The Streets," *Huffington Post*, March 20, 2013, https://www.huffingtonpost.com/2013/03/20/california-realignment-la-shootings-video_n_2916313.html.

236 Brian Day, "Ex-con accused in Christmas Day Pasadena slaying got early release," *Pasadena Star-News*, January 4, 2013, https://www.pasadenastarnews.com/2013/01/04/ex-con-accused-in-christmas-day-pasadena-slaying-got-early-release/

237 Justin Goss, Joseph Hayes, "California's Changing Prison Population," *Just the Facts*, (San Francisco: Public Policy Institute of California, February 2018).

238 Nina Totenberg, "High Court Rules Calif. Must Cut Prison Population," National Public Radio, May 23, 2011, https://www.npr.org/2011/05/23/136579580/california-is-ordered-to-cut-its-prison-population.

239 "California's overcrowded prisons: Gulags in the sun," *The Economist*, August 13, 2009, https://www.economist.com/united-states/2009/08/13/gulags-in-the-sun.

240 John Pomfret, "California Prison System In 'Crisis,' Governor Says," *The Washington Post*, June 27, 2006, http://www.washingtonpost.com/wp-dyn/content/article/2006/06/26/AR2006062601240.html.

241 Dean Misczynski, "Rethinking the State-Local Relationship: Corrections," Public Policy Institute of California, August 2011, http://www.ppic.org/content/pubs/report/R_811DMR.pdf.

242 Mia Bird, Ryken Grattet, Viet Nguyen, "Realignment and Recidivism in California," Public Policy Institute of California, December 2017, http://www.ppic.org/publication/realignment-and-recidivism-in-california/.

243 "The 2018-19 Budget: Governor's Criminal Justice Proposals," Legislative Analyst's Office, February 27, 2018, https://lao.ca.gov/reports/2018/3762/2018-19-crim-justice-proposals-022818.pdf

244 "The 2018-19 Budget: Governor's Criminal Justice Proposals," Legislative Analyst's Office, February 27, 2018, https://lao.ca.gov/reports/2018/3762/2018-19-crim-justice-proposals-022818.pdf.

245 California State Budget 2018-19, Enacted Budget Summary, California Department of Finance, June 2018, Page 57.

246 Scott Graves, Enrique Ruacho, "Steady Climb: State Corrections Spending In California," Budget Backgrounder, California Budget Project, September 2011, https://calbudgetcenter.org/wp-content/uploads/110914_Corrections_Spending_BB.pdf.

247 Magnus Lofstrom, Brandon Martin, "Public Safety Realignment: Impacts So Far," Public Policy Institute of California, September 2015, http://www.ppic.org/publication/public-safety-realignment-impacts-so-far/.

248 Ted Gest, "California Officials Say Prison Realignment Puts State on 'Right Track,'" *The Crime Report*, Center on Media Crime and Justice, John Jay College July 31, 2017, https://thecrimereport.org/2017/07/31/california-officials-say-prison-realignment-puts-state-on-right-track/.

249 Susan Turner, Terry Fain, and Shirley Hunt, *Public Safety Realignment in Twelve California Counties*, (Santa Monica, CA: Rand Corporation, 2015).

250 "Prison realignment: New Calif. law broadly defines 'low-level' offenses," KPCC and wire services, October 4, 2011, https://www.scpr.org/news/2011/10/04/29248/new-calif-law-broadens-definition-low-level-feloni/.

251 "Prison realignment: New Calif. law broadly defines 'low-level' offenses," KPCC and wire services, October 4, 2011, https://www.scpr.org/news/2011/10/04/29248/new-calif-law-broadens-definition-low-level-feloni/.

252 Dean Misczynski, "Rethinking the State-Local Relationship: Corrections," Public Policy Institute of California, August 2011, http://www.ppic.org/content/pubs/report/R_811DMR.pdf.

253 Charis Kubrin and Carroll Seron, eds., "The Great Experiment: Realigning Criminal Justice In California And Beyond," *The ANNALS of the American Academy of Political Science* 664, no. 1 (March 2016).

254 "Crime in California 2011," California Department of Justice, California Justice Information Services Division, Bureau of Criminal Information and Analysis, Criminal Justice Statistics Center, accessed October 29, 2018, https://oag.ca.gov/sites/all/files/agweb/pdfs/cjsc/publications/candd/cd11/cd11.pdf.

255 "Crime in California 2017," California Department of Justice, California Justice Information Services Division, Bureau of Criminal Information and Analysis, Criminal Justice Statistics Center, Table 2, July 9, 2018, https://openjustice.doj.ca.gov/downloads/pdfs/cd17.pdf.

256 "Crime in California 2017," California Department of Justice, California Justice Information Services Division, Bureau of Criminal Information and Analysis, Criminal Justice Statistics Center, Table 2, July 9, 2018, https://openjustice.doj.ca.gov/downloads/pdfs/cd17.pdf.

257 "Crime in California 2016," California Department of Justice, California Justice Information Services Division, Bureau of Criminal Information and Analysis, Criminal Justice Statistics Center, Table 2, accessed October 29, 2018, https://openjustice.doj.ca.gov/downloads/pdfs/cd16.pdf.

258 "Crime in California 2017," California Department of Justice, California Justice Information Services Division, Bureau of Criminal Information and Analysis, Criminal Justice Statistics Center, Table 2, July 9, 2018, https://openjustice.doj.ca.gov/downloads/pdfs/cd17.pdf.

259 Rina Palta, "California prison reform didn't cause crime increase, study finds," KPCC radio, February 18, 2018, https://www.scpr.org/news/2016/02/18/57729/study-cas-prison-reform-did-nt-cause-crime-increase/.

260 Rina Palta, "California prison reform didn't cause crime increase, study finds," KPCC radio, February 18, 2018, https://www.scpr.org/news/2016/02/18/57729/study-cas-prison-reform-did-nt-cause-crime-increase/.

261 Mia Bird, Ryken Grattet, Viet Nguyen, "Realignment and Recidivism in California," Public Policy Institute of California, December 2017, http://www.ppic.org/publication/realignment-and-recidivism-in-california/.

262 Noel Jones, "Thousands of Prison Inmates Are Being Released Into Local Communities," *Los Angeles Sentinel*, January 25, 2018, https://lasentinel.net/thousands-of-prison-inmates-are-being-released-into-local-communities.html.

263 Mike Balsamo, "Gang member accused in officer's slaying was on probation," Associated Press, February 22, 2017, https://www.dailymail.co.uk/wires/ap/article-4248184/Gang-member-accused-officers-slaying-probation.html.

264 Mike Balsamo, "Gang member accused in officer's slaying was on probation," Associated Press, February 22, 2017, https://www.dailymail.co.uk/wires/ap/article-4248184/Gang-member-accused-officers-slaying-probation.html.

265 Samuel Chamberlain, "California deputy killed at Sacramento hotel, two state troopers wounded," Fox News, August 30, 2017, https://www.foxnews.com/us/california-deputy-killed-at-sacramento-hotel-two-state-troopers-wounded.

266 Hollie McKay, "California deputy's murder blamed on Gov. Brown-backed prison reform," Fox News, September 12, 2017, https://www.foxnews.com/us/california-deputys-murder-blamed-on-gov-brown-backed-prison-reform.

267 Michael Rushford, "Study Paints A False Picture About Crime In California," Criminal Justice Legal Foundation, December 8, 2017, https://www.cjlf.org/releases/17-12.htm.

268   Michael Rushford, "Study Paints A False Picture About Crime In California," Criminal Justice Legal Foundation, December 8, 2017, https://www.cjlf.org/releases/17-12.htm.

269   Michael Rushford, "Study Paints A False Picture About Crime In California," Criminal Justice Legal Foundation, December 8, 2017, https://www.cjlf.org/releases/17-12.htm.

270   Michael Rushford, "Study Paints A False Picture About Crime In California," Criminal Justice Legal Foundation, December 8, 2017, https://www.cjlf.org/releases/17-12.htm.

271   Justin Goss, Joseph Hayes, "California's Changing Prison Population," *Just the Facts*, (San Francisco: Public Policy Institute of California, February 2018).

272   Associated Press, "California Prisoners Could Be Moved Out Of State Due To Overcrowding," January 8, 2014, https://www.kpbs.org/news/2014/jan/08/california-prisoners-could-be-moved-out-state-due-/.

273   Mia Bird and Shannon McConville, "Health Care for California's Jail Population," Public Policy Institute of California, June 2014, Endnote 16, http://www.ppic.org/publication/health-care-for-californias-jail-population/.

274   Associated Press, "At $75,560, housing a prisoner in California now costs more than a year at Harvard," June 4, 2017, http://www.latimes.com/local/lanow/la-me-prison-costs-20170604-htmlstory.html.

275   "What you need to know about Proposition 47," California Department of Corrections and Rehabilitation, accessed October 29, 2018, https://www.cdcr.ca.gov/news/prop47.html.

276   "What you need to know about Proposition 47," California Department of Corrections and Rehabilitation, accessed October 29, 2018, https://www.cdcr.ca.gov/news/prop47.html.

277   "What you need to know about Proposition 47," California Department of Corrections and Rehabilitation, accessed October 29, 2018, https://www.cdcr.ca.gov/news/prop47.html.

278   Sam Stanton, "Prop. 47 victory shows California embracing 'smart on crime' approach, supporters say," *Sacramento Bee*, February 4, 2016, https://www.sacbee.com/news/politics-government/election/article3591130.html.

279   "Board Awards $103m in Prop 47 Funds to Innovative Rehabilitative Programs," California Board of State and Community Corrections, June 8, 2017, http://bscc.ca.gov/downloads/6.8.17%20%20PR%20Prop%2047.pdf.

280   Sam Stanton, "Prop. 47 victory shows California embracing 'smart on crime' approach, supporters say," *Sacramento Bee*, February 4, 2016, https://www.sacbee.com/news/politics-government/election/article3591130.html.

281 Sam Stanton, "Prop. 47 victory shows California embracing 'smart on crime' approach, supporters say," *Sacramento Bee*, February 4, 2016, https://www.sacbee.com/news/politics-government/election/article3591130.html.

282 Erica Sandberg, "After Proposition 47: Crime and No Consequences in California," *National Review*, January 30, 2018, https://www.nationalreview.com/2018/01/californias-proposition-47-crime-and-no-consequences/.

283 Erica Sandberg, "After Proposition 47: Crime and No Consequences in California," *National Review*, January 30, 2018, https://www.nationalreview.com/2018/01/californias-proposition-47-crime-and-no-consequences/.

284 Erica Sandberg, "After Proposition 47: Crime and No Consequences in California," *National Review*, January 30, 2018, https://www.nationalreview.com/2018/01/californias-proposition-47-crime-and-no-consequences/.

285 Erica Sandberg, "After Proposition 47: Crime and No Consequences in California," *National Review*, January 30, 2018, https://www.nationalreview.com/2018/01/californias-proposition-47-crime-and-no-consequences/.

286 University of California, Irvine, School of Social Ecology, "Fact sheet: Proposition 47 and Crime," Charles Kubrin, Bradley Bartos, accessed October 29, 2018, https://www.ics.uci.edu/~sternh/courses/265/kubrin_bartos.pdf.

287 Magnus Lofstrom, Brandon Martin, "Corrections: California has reversed its long-term incarceration trend," *California's Future:* Public Policy Institute of California, January 2018, http://www.ppic.org/wp-content/uploads/r-118mlr.pdf.

288 Darrell Smith, "Teen convicted in Davis couple's death to get juvenile review," *Sacramento Bee*, March 6, 2018, https://www.sacbee.com/news/local/article203536974.html.

289 Darrell Smith, "Jurors watch video confession in Davis killings," *Sacramento Bee*, September 25, 2014, https://www.sacbee.com/news/local/crime/article2611417.html.

290 Lauren Keene, "Appellate ruling sends March homicide case back to court," *Davis Enterprise*, March 6, 2018.

291 "Teen who murdered Davis couple could be retried as a juvenile in Yolo County court," *Daily Democrat*, March 6, 2018, https://www.dailydemocrat.com/newsletter/180309917/.

292 Darrell Smith, "Aspiring serial killer won't get chance at early release, Yolo court rules," *The Sacramento Bee,* October 24, 2018, https://www.sacbee.com/latest-news/article220586120.html

293 Michele Hanisee, "Parole Board Uncomfortable with the Truth," *City Watch*, February 19, 2018, https://citywatchla.com/index.php/voices/14940-parole-board-uncomfortable-with-the-truth.

294 Michele Hanisee, "Meet the Violent Inmates Getting Released from Prison," Association of Deputy District Attorneys of Los Angeles County, accessed October 29, 2018, https://www.laadda.com/meet-violent-inmates-getting-released-prison/.

295 Board of Parole Hearings, California Department of Corrections and Rehabilitation, January 5, 2018

296 Hon. J. Richard Couzens and Hon. Tricia A. Bigelow, "Proposition 57: 'The Public Safety And Rehabilitation Act of 2016,'" Barrister Press, 2017, http://www.courts.ca.gov/documents/prop57-Parole-and-Credits-Memo.pdf.

297 Hon. J. Richard Couzens and Hon. Tricia A. Bigelow, "Proposition 57: 'The Public Safety And Rehabilitation Act of 2016,'" Barrister Press, 2017, http://www.courts.ca.gov/documents/prop57-Parole-and-Credits-Memo.pdf.

298 Marisa Lagos, "Brown Sees Proposition 57 as Key to Ending Court's Oversight of Prisons," The California Report, KQED News, September 12, 2016, https://www.kqed.org/news/11081078/gov-brown-sees-prop-57-as-key-to-ending-court-prison-oversight.

299 Marisa Lagos, "Brown Sees Proposition 57 as Key to Ending Court's Oversight of Prisons," The California Report, KQED News, September 12, 2016, https://www.kqed.org/news/11081078/gov-brown-sees-prop-57-as-key-to-ending-court-prison-oversight.

300 Editorial Board, "Prop 57 is a much-needed check on prosecutorial power. Vote yes," *Los Angeles Times*, October 5, 2016, http://www.latimes.com/opinion/editorials/la-ed-end-proposition-57-20161004-snap-story.html.

301 "Proposition 57: Criminal sentencing," *CALmatters,* September 28, 2016, https://calmatters.org/articles/proposition-57-criminal-sentencing/.

302 Editorial Board, "Proposition 57 a debacle for Jerry Brown because of potential early parole for sex offenders," *San Diego Union-Tribune*, February 12, 2018, http://www.sandiegouniontribune.com/opinion/editorials/sd-prop-57-sex-offenders-20180212-story.html.

303 Debra J. Saunders, "Proposition 57: Do you feel lucky," *San Francisco Chronicle*, October 21, 2016, https://www.sfchronicle.com/opinion/saunders/article/Proposition-57-Do-you-feel-lucky-10034282.php.

304 Debra J. Saunders, "Proposition 57: Do you feel lucky," *San Francisco Chronicle*, October 21, 2016, https://www.sfchronicle.com/opinion/saunders/article/Proposition-57-Do-you-feel-lucky-10034282.php.

305 Association of Deputy District Attorneys of Los Angeles County, "Proposition 57 Fact Sheet", accessed October 29, 2018, https://files.constantcontact.com/56a3ed5c401/46bfcab0-d7da-44d5-94a6-b69eb3050707.pdf.

306 Association of Deputy District Attorneys of Los Angeles County, "Proposition 57 Fact Sheet," accessed October 29, 2018, https://files.constantcontact.com/56a3ed5c401/46bfcab0-d7da-44d5-94a6-b69eb3050707.pdf.

307 Association of Deputy District Attorneys of Los Angeles County, "Proposition 57 Fact Sheet," accessed October 29, 2018, https://files.constantcontact.com/56a3ed5c401/46bfcab0-d7da-44d5-94a6-b69eb3050707.pdf.

308 California District Attorneys Association, "CDAA Analysis of The Public Safety & Rehabilitation Act of 2016 (Governor's Initiative)," February 10, 2016, https://www.cdaa.org/wp-content/uploads/for-press-CDAA-Ad-Hoc-Analysis-PSRA-2016-Revised-021016-3.docx

309 California District Attorneys Association, "CDAA Analysis of The Public Safety & Rehabilitation Act of 2016 (Governor's Initiative)," February 10, 2016, https://www.cdaa.org/wp-content/uploads/for-press-CDAA-Ad-Hoc-Analysis-PSRA-2016-Revised-021016-3.docx.

310 California District Attorneys Association, "CDAA Analysis of The Public Safety & Rehabilitation Act of 2016 (Governor's Initiative)," February 10, 2016, https://www.cdaa.org/wp-content/uploads/for-press-CDAA-Ad-Hoc-Analysis-PSRA-2016-Revised-021016-3.docx.

311 California District Attorneys Association, "CDAA Analysis of The Public Safety & Rehabilitation Act of 2016 (Governor's Initiative)," February 10, 2016, https://www.cdaa.org/wp-content/uploads/for-press-CDAA-Ad-Hoc-Analysis-PSRA-2016-Revised-021016-3.docx.

312 Pauline Repard, "Prop. 57 swings pendulum from 'warehousing' to early parole," *The San Diego Union-Tribune*, January 1, 2018, http://www.sandiegouniontribune.com/news/courts/sd-me-prop57-parole-20171228-story.html.

313 Pauline Repard, "Prop. 57 swings pendulum from 'warehousing' to early parole," *The San Diego Union-Tribune*, January 1, 2018, http://www.sandiegouniontribune.com/news/courts/sd-me-prop57-parole-20171228-story.html.

314 Associated Press, "California must consider earlier parole for sex offenders, judge rules," February 9, 2018, http://www.latimes.com/local/lanow/la-me-sex-offenders-20180209-story.html.

315 "California Proposition 57, Parole for Non-Violent Criminals and Juvenile Court Requirements," Ballotpedia, https://ballotpedia.org/California_Proposition_57,_Parole_for_Non-Violent_Criminals_and_Juvenile_Court_Trial_Requirements_(2016)#cite_note-order2-1, accessed October 29, 2018.

316 Associated Press, "California must consider earlier parole for sex offenders, judge rules," February 9, 2018, http://www.latimes.com/local/lanow/la-me-sex-offenders-20180209-story.html.

317   Associated Press, "California must consider earlier parole for sex offenders, judge rules," February 9, 2018, http://www.latimes.com/local/lanow/la-me-sex-offenders-20180209-story.html

318   "Initiative Measure To Be Submitted Directly To Voters," Office of California Attorney General, November 28, 2017, https://www.oag.ca.gov/system/files/initiatives/pdfs/17-0044%20%28Reducing%20Crime%29.pdf

319   Aaron Read and Randy Perry, "Capitol Beat – The Reducing Crime And Keeping California Safe Act," December 14, 2017, https://porac.org/2017/12/capitol-beat-reducing-crime-keeping-california-safe-act/.

320   "Reducing Crime and Keeping California Safe Act of 2018," Initiative Measure To Be Submitted Directly To Voters, Initiative # 17-044, Submitted to Office of the California Attorney General, November 28, 2017, https://oag.ca.gov/system/files/initiatives/pdfs/17-0044%20%28Reducing%20Crime%29.pdf.

321   California Legislative Analyst's Office, "Fiscal Impact Estimate Report of the Reducing Crime and Keeping California Safe Act," December 20, 2017, https://oag.ca.gov/system/files/initiatives/pdfs/fiscal-impact-estimate-report%2817-0044%29_0.pdf.

322   Garrett Seivold, "California Campaign Seeks to Fix Prop 47 by Making Serial Theft a Felony," *Loss Prevention Magazine*, December 7, 2017, https://losspreventionmedia.com/insider/shoplifting-organized-retail-crime/california-campaign-seeks-fix-prop-47-making-serial-theft-felony/.

323   Alexan Balekian, "Chief Dyer: We've Arrested A Person 83 Times Since Prop 47 Passed," KSEE-TV 24/KGPE-TV 47, July 26, 2018, https://www.yourcentralvalley.com/news/chief-dyer-we-ve-arrested-a-person-83-times-since-prop-47-passed/1327518371.

324   Don Thompson, "Judge: California must eye earlier parole for sex offenders," Associated Press, February 9, 2018, https://www.apnews.com/452114b8457a4d82b632f98b5099ef79.

325   Casey Tolan, "Is California closer to closing private prisons," *Daily Democrat*, February 4, 2019, https://www.dailydemocrat.com/2019/02/04/is-california-closer-to-closing-private-prisons/

326   Austill Stuart, "Private prisons are helping California and can be used to reduce prison population," *Orange County Register*, April 10, 2017, https://www.ocregister.com/2017/03/31/private-prisons-are-helping-california-and-can-be-used-to-reduce-prison-population/.

327   Austill Stuart, "Private prisons are helping California and can be used to reduce prison population," *Orange County Register*, April 10, 2017, https://www.ocregister.com/2017/03/31/private-prisons-are-helping-california-and-can-be-used-to-reduce-prison-population/.

328   Austill Stuart, "Private prisons are helping California and can be used to reduce prison popula-
         tion," *Orange County Register*, April 10, 2017, https://www.ocregister.com/2017/03/31/private-
         prisons-are-helping-california-and-can-be-used-to-reduce-prison-population/.

329   Associated Press, "At $75,560, housing a prisoner in California now costs more than a year at
         Harvard," June 4, 2017, http://www.latimes.com/local/lanow/la-me-prison-costs-20170604-ht-
         mlstory.html.

330   Associated Press, "California Prisoners Could Be Moved Out Of State Due To Overcrowding,"
         January 8, 2014, https://www.kpbs.org/news/2014/jan/08/california-prisoners-could-be-moved-
         out-state-due-/.

331   Assembly Bill 1320, Sess. of 2017 (Cal. 2013), https://leginfo.legislature.ca.gov/faces/billPdf.
         xhtml?bill_id=201720180AB1320&version=20170AB132094ENR.

332   Office of Governor Jerry Brown, Veto message of Assembly Bill 1320, October 5, 2017, https://
         www.gov.ca.gov/wp-content/uploads/2017/11/AB_1320_Veto_Message_2017.pdf.

333   California Legislative Information, AB-32 State prisons: private, for-profit administration ser-
         vices, https://leginfo.legislature.ca.gov/faces/billTextClient.xhtml?bill_id=201920200AB32

334   Sasha Volokh, "Don't end federal private prisons," *Washington Post*, August 19, 2016, https://
         www.washingtonpost.com/news/volokh-conspiracy/wp/2016/08/19/dont-end-federal-pri-
         vate-prisons/?noredirect=on&utm_term=.dc09f329ce01.

335   Sasha Volokh, "Don't end federal private prisons," *Washington Post*, August 19, 2016, https://
         www.washingtonpost.com/news/volokh-conspiracy/wp/2016/08/19/dont-end-federal-pri-
         vate-prisons/?noredirect=on&utm_term=.dc09f329ce01.

336   Judicial Council of California, Administrative Office of the Courts, Center for Families, Chil-
         dren & the Courts, "Balanced And Restorative Justice: An Information Manual For California,"
         2006, http://www.courts.ca.gov/documents/BARJManual3.pdf

337   Judicial Council of California, Administrative Office of the Courts, Center for Families, Chil-
         dren & the Courts, "Balanced And Restorative Justice: An Information Manual For California,"
         2006, http://www.courts.ca.gov/documents/BARJManual3.pdf.

338   Yolo County District Attorney's Office, "Neighborhood Court: A Restorative Justice Program,"
         https://yoloda.org/progressive-programs/neighborhood-court/

339   Yolo County District Attorney's Office, "Neighborhood Court 4-Year Report: An Analysis of
         Program Development, Challenges, and Achievements from 2013 to Present," Nicole Francis
         and Jake Whitaker, July 17, 2017, https://yoloda.org/wp-content/uploads/2014/01/NHC-4-yr-
         Report.pdf.

340 Bryan Caplan and Edward P. Stringham, "Privatizing the Adjudication of Disputes," *Journal of Alternative Dispute Resolution* 7, no. 4 (July 2008): 29-50.

341 Kerry Jackson, "Commentary: S.F. tries to stop private-sector second-chance program," *East Bay Times*, November 11, 2016, https://www.eastbaytimes.com/2016/11/11/commentary-s-f-tries-to-stop-private-sector-second-chance-program/.

342 Kerry Jackson, "Commentary: S.F. tries to stop private-sector second-chance program," *East Bay Times*, November 11, 2016, https://www.eastbaytimes.com/2016/11/11/commentary-s-f-tries-to-stop-private-sector-second-chance-program/.

343 Kerry Jackson, "Commentary: S.F. tries to stop private-sector second-chance program," *East Bay Times*, November 11, 2016, https://www.eastbaytimes.com/2016/11/11/commentary-s-f-tries-to-stop-private-sector-second-chance-program/.

344 "Our Locations," Walmart, last modified August 15, 2018, https://corporate.walmart.com/our-story/locations/united-states/california#/united-states/california.

345 Kerry Jackson, "Court Ruling Shuts Down Effective Private-Sector Restorative Justice Program," Pacific Research Institute *Right by the Bay* Blog, September 12, 2017, https://www.pacificresearch.org/court-ruling-shuts-down-effective-private-sector-restorative-justice-program/.

346 Kerry Jackson, "Court Ruling Shuts Down Effective Private-Sector Restorative Justice Program," Pacific Research Institute *Right by the Bay* Blog, September 12, 2017, https://www.pacificresearch.org/court-ruling-shuts-down-effective-private-sector-restorative-justice-program/.

347 Kerry Jackson, "Court Ruling Shuts Down Effective Private-Sector Restorative Justice Program," Pacific Research Institute *Right by the Bay* Blog, September 12, 2017, https://www.pacificresearch.org/court-ruling-shuts-down-effective-private-sector-restorative-justice-program/.

348 Kerry Jackson, "Court Ruling Shuts Down Effective Private-Sector Restorative Justice Program," Pacific Research Institute *Right by the Bay* Blog, September 12, 2017, https://www.pacificresearch.org/court-ruling-shuts-down-effective-private-sector-restorative-justice-program/.

349 Kerry Jackson, "Court Ruling Shuts Down Effective Private-Sector Restorative Justice Program," Pacific Research Institute *Right by the Bay* Blog, September 12, 2017, https://www.pacificresearch.org/court-ruling-shuts-down-effective-private-sector-restorative-justice-program/.

350 David Washburn, "San Diego Tries Restorative Justice in a Traumatized Community," *California Health Report*, November 27, 2017, https://www.calhealthreport.org/2017/11/27/san-diego-tries-restorative-justice-traumatized-community/.

351 David Washburn, "San Diego Tries Restorative Justice in a Traumatized Community," *California Health Report*, November 27, 2017, https://www.calhealthreport.org/2017/11/27/san-diego-tries-restorative-justice-traumatized-community/.

352 David Washburn, "San Diego Tries Restorative Justice in a Traumatized Community," *California Health Report*, November 27, 2017, https://www.calhealthreport.org/2017/11/27/san-diego-tries-restorative-justice-traumatized-community/.

353 "Shirley You Jest – Stanford Sexual Assault," Michele Hanisee, Association of Deputy District Attorneys for Los Angeles County, posted June 16, 2016, https://www.laadda.com/shirley-you-jest-stanford-sexual-assault/.

354 Assembly Rules Committee, Bill analysis of Assembly Bill 2590, August 19, 2016.

355 Dan Walters, "The crime debate continues, and bail reform will be next," *CALmatters*, December 13, 2017, https://calmatters.org/articles/commentary/commentary-crime-debate-continues-bail-reform-will-next/.

356 Dan Walters, "The crime debate continues, and bail reform will be next," *CALmatters*, December 13, 2017, https://calmatters.org/articles/commentary/commentary-crime-debate-continues-bail-reform-will-next/.

357 Judicial Council of California letter to Assemblyman Reginald B. Jones-Sawyer Jr., chair of the Assembly Public Safety Committee, June 30, 2017

358 Kerry Jackson, "Lawmakers should think carefully before leashing 'The Dog,'" *Orange County Register*, May 12, 2017, https://www.ocregister.com/2017/05/12/lawmakers-should-think-carefully-before-leashing-the-dog/.

359 Kerry Jackson, "Lawmakers should think carefully before leashing 'The Dog,'" *Orange County Register*, May 12, 2017, https://www.ocregister.com/2017/05/12/lawmakers-should-think-carefully-before-leashing-the-dog/.

360 Marc Klass, "California bail reform bill may be trendy, but it would hurt victims' rights," *Sacramento Bee*, March 28, 2018, https://www.sacbee.com/opinion/california-forum/article207085264.html.

Acknowledgements

Thanks to Sally Pipes, president and CEO of the Pacific Research Institute, and Rowena Itchon, PRI senior vice president, for giving me the opportunity to write this book, and to contribute to PRI's Center for California Reform. I'm also grateful to PRI's Director of Communications Tim Anaya, who provided the benefits of his experience working on criminal justice issues in the Capitol, and for his tireless editing. Thanks, as well, are due to PRI senior fellow Lance Izumi for helping me realize how profoundly crime impacts education, and Dana Beigel, whose graphic design talents put all the pieces together into a readable format.

About the Author

KERRY JACKSON

KERRY JACKSON is an independent journalist and opinion writer with extensive experience covering politics and public policy. Currently a Fellow with the Center for California Reform at the Pacific Research Institute (PRI), Kerry writes weekly op-eds and blog posts on statewide issues and occasional policy papers. In 2017, he wrote *Unaffordable: How Government Made California's Housing Shortage a Crisis and How Free Market Ideas Can Restore Affordability and Supply,* an issue brief on California's housing crisis which won bipartisan praise. He spent 18 years writing editorials on domestic and foreign policy for *Investor's Business Daily* and three years as the assistant director of public affairs for the American Legislative Exchange Council. His work has appeared in the *New York Observer,* the *Orange County Register, The Freeman, Forbes,* and on *Fox & Hounds Daily* and *Real Clear Markets.* He has written for the American Media Institute and Real Clear Investigations, and edited "The Growth Manifesto" for the Committee to Unleash Prosperity. A graduate of Georgia State University, Kerry has also served as a public affairs consultant for the George Mason University School of Law and worked as a reporter and editor for local newspapers in the metro Atlanta and northern Virginia regions.

About Pacific Research Institute

The Pacific Research Institute (PRI) champions freedom, opportunity, and personal responsibility by advancing free-market policy solutions. It provides practical solutions for the policy issues that impact the daily lives of all Americans, and demonstrates why the free market is more effective than the government at providing the important results we all seek: good schools, quality health care, a clean environment, and a robust economy.

Founded in 1979 and based in San Francisco, PRI is a non-profit, non-partisan organization supported by private contributions. Its activities include publications, public events, media commentary, community leadership, legislative testimony, and academic outreach.